THE

QUEEN ISABELLA

CAUSEWAY

COLLAPSE

THE
QUEEN ISABELLA
CAUSEWAY
COLLAPSE

JUAN CARMONA
AND ROBERT ESPERICUETA

THE
History
PRESS

Published by The History Press
Charleston, SC
www.historypress.com

First published 2024

Manufactured in the United States

ISBN 9781467156813

Library of Congress Control Number: 2024937698

Notice: The information in this book is true and complete to the best of our knowledge. It is offered without guarantee on the part of the authors or The History Press. The authors and The History Press disclaim all liability in connection with the use of this book.

CONTENTS

CONTENTS

PART I

1
WHO ARE WE REALLY?

What exactly is the true measure of a man, and exactly when does one become a man? Removing any masculine reference, the same questions can be posed: What does it mean to be a human being on this planet filled with billions of other human beings? In what way does our true nature reveal itself, and how do we display our humanity? These are questions that at times call for self-reflection but other times are demonstrated by our actions, especially the actions that are a response to the outside influences of the world.

For sure, we show our humanity in our interactions with family members, taking care of each other and having them take care of us. From the moment a parent holds their child for the first time until the moment when their children hold them for the last time, we are interconnected; we survive and grow in these familial connections. Then come our friends, some acquaintances, some as close as family—indeed many are considered part of the greater family. We grow and evolve with them, experiencing life together. Sometimes these friendships end with our youth, and other times they continue into adulthood. However, through all of the above, we reveal different aspects of ourselves to each other, reach out for help and extend a hand in assistance. These relationships both with our family and friends reveal something of who we are and our humanity.

Now just what does humanity mean? *Merriam-Webster Dictionary* defines *humanity* as "compassionate, sympathetic, or generous behavior or disposition: the quality or state of being humane."[1] Those terms probably describe one's day-to-day interactions with family, friends and co-workers. How we interact with these concentric circles of our social network reveals a great portion of our humanity to the world. The respect we give to each other as we speak, work, interact and serve one another reveals our humanity and our empathy to others. The stark fact is that we have empathy toward people we know because we know them, their thoughts, dreams, triumphs, tragedies, loves and heartbreaks, all of which give us our empathy for these individuals.

However, there is another level to our humanity, one that if we are lucky, we never really have to demonstrate and that is a response to a crisis involving complete strangers. We see this type of humanity on full display during natural disasters like Hurricane Katrina and national tragedies like that of 9/11, an event whose shadow will loom throughout this story. What happened during those two major events would involve thousands of victims and thousands of responders. All acted selflessly trying to assist and save their fellow man. Most of them were first responders trained to assist with emergencies, but it can be said that they were not mentally prepared, nor could they imagine the depths of tragedy in which they would become active actors. Courage, empathy and strength of character were at the forefront. These men and women used their skills, training, and bravery to show humanity what humanity really was.

Humanity takes on another hue when the events are isolated and experienced by a small group of people, strangers and friends who by circumstances of fate are thrust into a tragedy that is beyond them or any type of previous experience both personal and professional. In this story, humanity is revealed in four young men, all in their early twenties, all

From left to right: Roland Lee Moya, Robert Espericueta, Antonio Salinas Jr. and Leroy Moya. *Courtesy of Robert Espericueta.*

barely beginning their own adult lives. On that fateful night, those young men revealed their humanity and their love for their fellow man. Their eyes searched through the dark night using only a small spotlight and their ears as they struggled to hear the cries of the victims over the sound of cascading water, the roar of their boat's engine and the splashing of the waves against their boat. They were filled with adrenaline, fear and anxiety, and their hearts swelled with hope, hope that they could save a life, make a difference and at the same time survive that night. Surviving, because in the back of everyone's minds on that night, September 15, 2001, just after 9/11, they knew not whether they were wading into a terrorist event. Indeed, on that night, the meaning of humanity was demonstrated by four young men on a small boat, in a big ocean.

2
ACCIDENT PROLOGUE

The story presented in this book has been brewing in a pot held closed by a rigid twenty-year lid, a lid made up of fear, anxiety, distrust and hope—hope that by the time the story came to light, many of its main actors would be forgotten along with their roles in this tragic affair. Indeed, some of the people mentioned in this story have since passed, some by their own hands. Others who were involved have moved on with their lives, carrying a dark cloud of memories of that sad day. Sights such as car taillights and the smell of gasoline bring to the forefront memories that are always hovering over every waking moment of their lives. Some still go to South Padre Island, instinctively rolling down their windows, just in case. Residents of the area instinctively do the same due to a latent uneasiness that comes with the knowledge that the spiraling Queen Isabella Causeway was once laid low.

In some sense, this story comes to you due to another national tragedy compounded by the Texas disaster: the COVID pandemic, a time of extreme isolation for many Americans. We were separated from our loved ones, especially our elders. For many Americans, loss was a fact of daily life, from loss of freedom of movement to loss of employment and the most extreme type of loss, death. There is probably not a single American who did not experience loss either directly or indirectly. As we were driven inward into our homes, we sought out escapist entertainment, stories that took us away from ourselves. For some it was diving deep into the Netflix catalogue, finding shows like *Tiger King*, which one could argue would never have found as much success had it not been for the pandemic. However, in the tight-knit Rio Grande Valley community, many residents turned to the reexamination of an event that they thought they knew about, but now the true story is finally being told.

The story emerged and was produced in the midst of the pandemic and during the winter storm of February 2021: a production by Joshua Moroles with the initial episodes relating the firsthand account of Robert Espericueta, the captain of the boat that rescued the only survivors of the collapse. At the time of this writing, the podcast and video of the podcast have over 100,000 listens/views. According to the Texas State Comptrollers' Office,

Joshua Moroles. *Courtesy of Joshua Moroles.*

as of the last census, the population of the Rio Grande Valley is currently at 2.4 million residents; to have over 100,000 people listening to the podcast reveals the enormous interest in the story.[2] Undoubtedly, these residents were struck by the fact that they had not really heard the story, and word of mouth probably drove the listenership. As we all sat in our homes (or, if you were like me, outside), we were drawn in by Robert's booming voice and his natural ability to tell a story that was both engaging and honest.

The podcast was the production of Joshua Moroles. Josh is a Valley native born in Weslaco, Texas, who has lived in San Juan, Mercedes and Pharr and currently lives in McAllen. Moroles is an entrepreneur who works in digital marketing. His path to his current career began at the age of thirty, when he was working at a Dairy Queen his father owned in Mercedes. He stated, "I was serving a customer at the window, and they said that they were on their lunch break. It occurred to me at that moment when I was thirty years old that I had never had a lunch break anywhere else other than Dairy Queen."[3] He refers to it as a very self-reflective moment in his life. He left his father's restaurant and embarked on a humanitarian mission in the Dominican Republic. From there, he sought out engagement in a world beyond Dairy Queen and found his way to Facebook advertising when it was in its infancy and the public was not too sure about it or how it worked, but he saw the potential of this new medium.

After a year of working in the digital marketing field, he was approached by a friend to join in a business venture. The firm became successful, but in the end, he was pushed out and decided to continue on his own. He obtained ten digital marketing certificates, and for the past five years has been a "solopreneur" constantly staying on top of the new digital tools and social media. Moroles said of his career,

> I just find it very easy because I learn quick if I can get my hands on something, I can learn it fast, and it'll stay in my head. So, the more I focus on it, the better I'll get at it, and I'll get exponentially better at it. I got all my technical certificates, and ever since then, I started making videos. I hated waiting for the video guy to give me his content because that pushed everything back, and I hated for the photographer to take forever to edit. So, I just learned it all. I became a one-stop shop, which is weird for companies because they're used to hiring big teams. And then I can turn around, do the same things, and for a fraction of the time since I'm one person.[4]

Picture from Robert's business House Club Poker and Lounge. *Courtesy of Juan Carmona.*

He also began to work on podcasts, using them both as a marketing tool and to provide information to his audience; then came a chance to meet with Robert.

Joshua first met Robert Espericueta at the poker club Robert owned in Edinburg, Texas. Robert gave him a tour of the business, and Joshua noticed a lot of memorabilia around the bridge collapse. There was a key to the city and a congratulatory plaque, and when Josh asked about them, Robert briefly told him the story of the bridge collapse, nothing too detailed at the time. They did not really stay in touch; however, sometime later, Robert sent Joshua a message on Facebook, explaining that there was something he wanted to do, as the twentieth anniversary of the bridge collapse was coming up. At first, Josh ignored it. Robert messaged him one more time, telling him that if he didn't get this off his chest, he was just going to shelve it, Josh relented and went to visit Robert in his office. Of that meeting, Josh said, "He tells me the story, and for an hour and a half, I'm just sitting there compelled by what he told me because he was and is a very good storyteller. So, I said, right after that, 'Let's do it, let's go full steam,'" and the podcast was born.[5]

3

THE BRIDGE

The Queen Isabella Causeway snakes its way from the city of Port Isabel to South Padre Island. It rises and falls like a slow roller coaster from the mainland to the island. Today the bridge sees over nine million cars drive across it every year.[6] These cars carry everyone from locals from the mainland to those who live on the island and tourists who come from all over the world to visit this little vacation hotspot located in the South Texas region called the Rio Grande Valley, RGV or simply the Valley for those who live there. For some visitors, it is the only part of the Valley that they know, and for most residents, it is the sight they see that lets them know that they are home.

The drive to South Padre Island takes you through the city of Los Fresnos via Highway 100. For those who are in the know, Los Fresnos is a speed trap, and you can see all the traffic immediately slow down as you come into the city limits and then speed back up as soon as they get out of city limits. The drive out from the city limits lets you know that you are beginning to get close to the ocean, as sand begins to appear on either side of the road and at times pockets of water are visible in the distance.

South Padre Island's history is as long and as storied as the bridge itself. Geographically, the island is a barrier island that provides some protection for the mainland shoreline. Geologists estimate the island is one thousand years old. Another aspect of the island's geography that may have played a role on the fateful night of September 15, 2001, is that according to the National Park Service, "Padre Island is in a constant state of change,

The Queen Isabella Causeway. *Courtesy of Joshua Moroles.*

moved by gentle Gulf breezes, violent tropical storms and hurricanes, and the rhythmic ebb and flow of tides and crashing waves. Beach, dunes, grasslands, and tidal flats are shaped and reshaped daily, a constant reminder of just how fragile our Island environment can be."[7] It is this violent churning from winds and the strong tides pushed from a storm miles away that made their way into the Laguna Madre (the name of the body of water between the island and the mainland) and played a major role in the September 15 disaster.

The first inhabitants of the island were the Karankawa, a tribe whose homeland ranged along the waterways of South Texas. They migrated from the coastal islands inland into Texas to sustain themselves through fishing and hunting all manner of game that was once plentiful, from bison to deer.[8] They were known for being exceptionally tall; in fact, some Spanish sources place them at seven feet tall—even if this is a bit of an exaggeration, this description lets you know how the Spanish viewed them. The other ancient inhabitants, which you can still go see today, are the famous sea turtles that have made their way onto the shores of Texas's barrier islands for centuries. Five distinct species can be found on the islands: loggerhead, leatherback, hawksbill, green and, the most prevalent, the Ridley sea turtle. Their presence has become part of South Padre Island's tourist industry with the establishment of Sea Turtle Inc., which performs a variety of services, from rehabilitation of sea turtles to conservation and educational services. Sea Turtle Inc. offers field trips and educational materials; one can also visit the site and see the turtles.

The first European settlement of the island was under a Spanish land grant via King Charles III to Nicolas Ballí in 1759. The grant would make its way to Ballí's grandson José Nicolás Ballí, who led the first permanent settlement on the island. He went on to establish a Catholic church on the island and not only ministered to the people of the settlement but also attempted to Christianize the Karankawa residents of the island. José Ballí is the namesake of the island: initially called La Isla Padre, it eventually became South Padre Island. In time, the island would grow into the tourist destination it has become and at the same time see its share of tragedy and triumph.

When it comes to tourism, one of the most popular times of the year for visiting the island is spring break. In the 1960s, Fort Lauderdale, Florida, was the place to be when it came to spring break. Nonetheless, teenagers who came back home to the Valley from their various universities and local colleges and high school students who could not afford a Fort Lauderdale vacation began gathering at the island instead. A practice that began on Easter break soon stretched into spring break. The early hangout used to be the Sandy Retreat Hotel, where students would gather. In time, bands began to set up and the road was even closed to traffic so that the party could be expanded. In time, friends of friends began to invite students from all over the country to South Padre Island, and this gradually evolved into the spring break we see today.

Another aspect that attracted teenagers from across the country is South Padre Island's proximity to Mexico, specifically Matamoros, Tamaulipas. You could certainly obtain a beer or a drink from the vast number of parties occurring in many hotel rooms or condos on the island or from someone on the beach. If you were under twenty-one and wanted to experience a club or a bar, unrestricted, Mexico is the place to go. Not to mention, traveling to Mexico was also an experience that many spring breakers wanted to enjoy while they were in South Texas.

The burgeoning population and the increasing number of people who visited the island eventually led to the need for a bridge to provide easy access on and off the island. Initially, the first bridge project saw several starts and stops. Originally, the bridge was part of the idea of a scenic drive down from Galveston Island to South Padre Island dreamed up by State Park Board member D.E. Culp; however, financing was not found, and the project was shelved. Nevertheless, the need and the idea for one did not go away.

In 1930, the General Electric and Development Company of New York City was awarded a $1.5 million contract to build not only a bridge but also a 150-room hotel at the end of the bridge. With financial backing coming from New York senator John Hastings and his cohorts, the bridge seemed like a done deal, but the Great Depression—which had already begun creating economic havoc in the United States—took its toll on the senator and his investors. The plans once again fell through, and the bridge remained on hold.

The year 1950 would see the approval of an $850,000 bond for a causeway. As part of the bond put forth by State Senator Rogers Kelley, a tollbooth would be installed, and the tolls would be used to pay for the cost of the bridge, which was tallied at $2 million. On July 7, 1953, a barge rammed one of the towers of the bridge, bringing down two pylons and foreshadowing a much more tragic event in 2001. On November 14, 1954, after the completion of repairs and the earthen parts of the causeway, the bridge was once again open for traffic. The age of large-scale tourism had begun; by August 20, 1954, the bridge celebrated 100,000 people who had crossed it and paid the toll. One can almost imagine if there was still a toll to cross the bridge, the gridlock of traffic would be unimaginable. Thankfully, toll collection ended on March 1, 1968.

June 26, 1966, saw yet another collision with the bridge by a group of barges, but repairs were quickly conducted for the bridge to be reopened a few hours later. Then in 1967, one of the strongest hurricanes to hit South Texas, Hurricane Beulah, blew through the causeway as it was on its way to wreak havoc on the Valley. The storm caused cracks in the concrete that held up the bridge and created huge potholes throughout the bridge.

The damages the bridge sustained were so significant that in 1969, plans for a new, larger bridge were drawn up. This version of the Queen Isabella Causeway opened for traffic in 1974 at a cost of $12 million. The bridge was built north of the old swing bridge, which is in still use, and was passed by the barge that would collapse the bridge in 2001. At a span of 15,272 feet, the causeway is the longest bridge in Texas—its design has it curving up and down and was made to protect it from any number of hurricanes that make their way across the bay into the Rio Grande Valley. The causeway has been hit throughout the years by barges large and small, but none of the incidents were as violent as what happened in 2001. Nevertheless, it's not just barges that collide with the bridge: in 1996 another vehicle struck the causeway.[9]

On August 13, 1996, a Cessna TR182 Turbo Skylane RG struck the causeway at 6:22 p.m. According to the National Transportation Board (NTSB), the probable cause was "pilot impairment of judgment and performance due to alcohol and drugs, and failure of the pilot(s) to maintain obstacle clearance, during an intentional low altitude flight maneuver (low pass under a bridge)." Witnesses reported that the plane flew underneath the bridge from the north side to the south side, and when it came around for another pass, instead of passing through, it struck one of the causeway's pylons and fell into the water. Investigators found both the vertical and horizontal stabilizers in the bridge. Both men died in the crash; they were both found to be pilots. Autopsies on both revealed that the pilot's blood contained both alcohol and cocaine and the passenger possessed marijuana and cocaine. The witness testimony and the toxicology report were what the NTSB used to draw this conclusion.[10] The impact did more damage to the plane than it did to the bridge, revealing both the strength of the bridge and just how hard the bridge was hit by *Brown Water V* in the early morning hours of September 15, 2001.

As of late, talk of having another bridge built, which was elevated during the time of the accident, has been growing louder. In an interview, Kevin Medders, environmental development chairman, was quoted in July 2021 stating, "There's more movement and now with the proposal to update the environmental study, it will be a player in the game. The life expectancy of the bridge, we're 8 years into when it expired and the incident with the barge several years ago opened their eyes to the fact that we only have a point of entry."[11] Truly, the fact that he references the tragedy of the collapse that took place twenty years ago, yet the need for a second bridge is still a "study" reveals that the island may need something more stark to drive the construction of a new bridge. Nevertheless, South Texas continues to grow, and tourism will undoubtedly be on the rise as the pandemic subsides. The story of the collapse shows that safety needs to be at the forefront of these conversations because traffic continues both in the water and in the air.

4
9/11

There is no way of telling this story without talking about an earlier event that pervades just about every aspect of what happened that fateful night, 9/11. Students born after this seminal event in U.S. history have known nothing else other than the post-9/11 world. Indeed, for those of us who lived through it, the passage of time has made us somewhat disconnected from the anxiety that invaded everyday life in America. There was fear that we were in the middle of a war, unlike any other war that America had ever been involved in, in modern times—a war that was being carried out within the borders of the United States.

The last war fought on American soil was the Civil War, which ended in 1865. The wars that followed, from the Spanish-American War to World War II, Korea, Vietnam, and so forth, were always fought away from America's shores. The fear and anxiety that came with those wars were very different; they were connected more to the fear of being drafted or that your loved ones would be and then went on to become the very real concern that they may die in combat. There was never the thought that war would come to the homeland. In a sense, we knew that we had the greatest army in the world, and although we may lose men, we had no fear that our borders would be breached by our enemies or that we would have to fight it collectively and actively ourselves. This is the very situation that Americans found themselves in after September 11, 2001. The "enemy" had breached our shores; they were and could be anywhere.

A Brief Reflection on 9/11

September 11, 2001, was a clear, crisp Tuesday morning. Everyone was going about their day in the North Tower of the World Trade Center when at 8:45 a.m. American Airlines Flight 11, a Boeing 767 containing over twenty thousand pounds of jet fuel (the flight was picked by the hijackers because it was going cross country and would be heavily laden with fuel), hit the tower, smashing deep into the building, floors ninety-three through ninety-nine. It immediately ignited those floors, and the flames started to make their way up toward the top floors. From the onset, there was confusion about what had happened; for the most part, reports related that it was some kind of accident, and they were attempting to find out what had caused the accident. However, that narrative changed eighteen minutes later when United Airlines Flight 175, another Boeing 767, hit the South Tower of the World Trade Center around the sixtieth floor. At that point, everyone knew that there was some sort of coordination going on; the question became who was responsible, and the fear of what's next began to set into the American consciousness. This fear set in deeper when at 9:45 a.m. American Airlines Flight 77 crashed headlong into the Pentagon. A fourth plane was also hijacked that day, United Flight 93.

In the past, planes had certainly been hijacked before, but never had they literally been used as weapons. So for the most part, people on board hijacked planes waited to see if demands were fulfilled and/or where they would be taken. This was probably on the minds of most of those aboard the planes that struck the Twin Towers and the Pentagon; however, by the time Flight 93 was taken, the passengers had learned of the fate of the other planes. They were determined not to go down without a fight, put up a heroic resistance and eventually forced the hijackers to crash the plane into the countryside and not a populated target.

As all this was taking place, more tragedy was unfolding for the residents of New York City and the nation. Forty minutes after being struck—from the enormous heat from the fires fed by jet fuel, plus the pressure of the weight of the above floors—the South Tower collapsed in dramatic fashion, pancaking down on the floors below and bringing the whole structure down. Then at 10:30 a.m., the whole situation repeated itself. The North Tower collapsed as well. The collapse of these buildings sent an enormous cloud of debris, smoke and ash down all around the surrounding area and on the people who were nearby. The fall of the towers killed 2,606 people, including rescue workers who were desperately trying to save as many people as they could. One of the eeriest scenes to come out of the tragedy came shortly after the collapse: in the silence brought on by shock and disbelief, there were the sounds of hundreds of emergency beacons, which first responders wear, chirping their wearers lost in the tragedy. In total, counting those lost in the towers, the Pentagon and the occupants of Flight 93, the terrorist attack killed 2,977 people, including the terrorists. What was also lost that day was the feeling of safety, that no war would come to our shores. The belief that wars were always fought "over there" was gone; the war had come to America.

The fact that there was no invading army that you could recognize by their uniforms, their columns marching, heavy tanks rolling down the street, the attack had come from a group of individuals, not a nation, made the anxiety in the air all the thicker. This meant that the enemy could be anywhere, and any innocuous object could be deadly. A backpack left unattended suddenly took on an ominous air. The attackers had used box cutters, not conventional weapons, which added to the fear that the enemy could be anywhere and attack out of nowhere. For days afterward people lived with the attacks; they were all over the television.

A study by the Pew Research Center lays out some stark numbers. Shortly after the attacks, 71 percent of those polled felt depressed and 49 percent had difficulty concentrating. The study goes on to point out that 90 percent percent of people saw and/or learned about the attacks through television and around 5 percent via the internet. One more telling statistic revealed in the study is that 87 percent of those polled felt angry about the attacks and 45 percent of the American population was worried about another attack.[12] The above facts lay out the psyche of Americans at the time. This was in a sense a shared experience; the attack occurred before the proliferation of the internet and social media. Cable news provided some outside news sources, but for the most part, the television news was still dominated by the big 3: ABC, NBC and CBS. Additionally, because most of what was happening was being watched in real time, with no time to add any real kind of spin, we did not see the immediate emergence of conspiracy theories that would come later. As a result, everyone saw the same things unfold, with the news personalities as much as in shock as their viewers.

Aside from the attacks, what else did Americans see? They saw the president being spirited away and spending some time in the air in Air Force One. The Capitol and other federal buildings were evacuated in Washington, D.C. For the first time in history, all aircraft were forced onto the ground. Fighter jets were scrambled to protect Air Force One and Washington, D.C. Eventually, the president addressed the nation, telling the American people that we had been attacked. All these events, almost all of which were unprecedented, accumulated in the consciousness of Americans. The impact on Americans who were watching these events unfold "collectively" is pointed out by psychologist Roxane Cohen Silver, PhD. In an interview with the American Psychological Association, she said,

> We were surprised to see the potent effect of media exposure on people's psychological and physical health over time. We argued that individuals did not have to be directly exposed to the events of 9/11, that is they did not need to be at the World Trade Center or around the buildings, to have been impacted by the events of 9/11....Well, what we did was look at individuals who indicated that they watched the attacks live on television. Those who can remember those days know that the second plane hit the World Trade Center and that was broadcast live. And individuals could also see the buildings fall live on television. We could juxtapose those individuals who said that they had seen the attacks live on television as compared to those who did not. We found that those who did witness the events of 9/11 live on television were more likely to be exhibiting stress responses, both psychological and physical stress responses, and more likely to develop physical health complaints over the next three years.[13]

Cohen Silver's assessment of the psychological trauma experienced by those who viewed the events either in person or on television and the Pew Research Center's numbers point out just how influential the event was to the people who lived through it and demonstrate the mindset of most Americans. This collective shock was rooted in the fear of the unknown. Who had attacked? Will there be more? Where will the next attack be? Who will do it? Why hadn't the authorities known? If they could not stop something this big, how can they possibly stop another? On the other hand, we had authorities—federal, state, county, city and military—in charge of the protection of citizens also asking the very same questions. Only when it comes to them, they felt not only the same shock but also a sense of failure. The failure was maybe not their own but of the system they worked in or those above them who were supposed to give them the tools, "intelligence," so that they could properly fulfill their duty. It would be years later before the failures were examined and the whole story was laid out for the American people and their protectors, but in the days after the attack, all branches of law enforcement were hypervigilant.

Both law enforcement and ordinary citizens jumped on anything that they perceived as a possible attack. One instance is highlighted by Garrett M. Graff, author of *The Only Plane in the Sky: An Oral History of 9/11*:

> The world suddenly looked scary to ordinary citizens—and even worse behind the closed doors of intelligence briefings…. According to one report soon after 9/11, a nuclear bomb that terrorists had managed to smuggle into the country was hidden on a train somewhere between Pittsburgh and Philadelphia. This tip turned out to have come from an informant who had misheard a conversation between two men in a bathroom in Ukraine—in other words, from a terrible global game of telephone. For weeks after, Bush would ask in briefings, "Is this another Ukrainian urinal incident?"[14]

There were countless similar incidents shortly after the attack, tales of suspicious white vans and sadly the singling out of people of Middle Eastern descent. Everyone was on edge, and everything the least out of the ordinary or sometimes normal mundane things did take on a more ominous hue.

This was the state of the world in the early morning hours of September 15, 2021, when a barge struck the Queen Isabella Causeway, bringing down a section of the bridge and killing eight people. It is what caused the hesitation of Robert and his companions. It also informed how authorities and first responders attended to the accident. It affected the witnesses who called 911 and explained why the four rescuers who found themselves in an impossible situation also found themselves being interrogated for hours by Texas Rangers. Everyone was scared, and much like 9/11, it would take some time before the accident was fully understood. As Robert put it, the collapse of the causeway was the "9/11 for the Rio Grande Valley." His reference was not that it was a similar terrorist attack, because it was not, but that it had a similar effect. The bridge is the largest man-made structure in the Valley, and it is something that every resident of South Texas takes for granted as part of the landscape of our lives. To see something like that laid low was a shock to most, and within the early hours of the collapse, it was certainly framed by many as just another attack on our American society. For many, the anxiety that was already in the air was amplified until the whole story unfolded. Sadly, the full extraordinary story is just now coming to the public view in its complete form.

PART II

5

THE ACCIDENT

Robert Espericueta was born in 1979 and raised in Mission, Texas. He comes from a family of six—one brother and two sisters—and went to school in La Joya but dropped out of high school when he was fourteen years old to work with his father, subdividing real estate. Robert's father bought land and plotted it out; installed the water, the sewer and the storm drainage; paved it; and put in the curb and gutters for the roads. Then he would sell the lots owner-financed. Robert described his business:

So my dad taught me that trade, and soon after that we were building homes on the lots we were subdividing and selling those as well. So, by the time I was eighteen, nineteen, I had built several homes on my own. My dad would go to the bank and sign over a residential lot to me as a sixteen-year-old minor and he would pledge the lot. I'd get a loan to build what-what is referred to as a spec home on the lot. Improving the bank's collateral and then we'd sell it. The bank would get paid, my dad's lot would get paid for and whatever money that we made, I would profit. I was introduced to the banking system very early in life and because of that and because of what I was learning and what I was becoming a part of, in terms of business, I was able to afford a brand-new boat in 2001, which led me to be under the bridge. Most thought that the boat belonged to my father or was a family boat. By the

Robert Espericueta. *Courtesy of Joshua Moroles.*

time 2001 came around, my wife and my newborn son and I were living in our very own home already. I had a Harley Davidson brand-new 2001, a brand-new boat and a brand-new pickup truck living in a new home because back then, the banking system wasn't what it is today. Back then I referred to it as the days of "milk and honey," when all you needed was

your signature, a handshake and a good plan, and you were
awarded the bank's trust and money, and you were allowed to
thrive. So, because of all those circumstances and the life I
was leading let me be able to be under the bridge that night.

That day, 9/11 anxiety hung in the air and was certainly on Robert's
mind when he began to organize a fishing trip with his cousins. They
were trying to find some return to normalcy in their lives and take their
minds off the continuous news coverage, which did not help everyone's
anxiety levels. By this point, the story was still being pieced together, the
investigations were active and speculations ran rampant. People were
slowly creeping out into their lives, their eyes, ears and minds on constant
high alert. Robert felt some time with his cousins on the boat he had just
recently purchased would do them all some good and at least provide a
distraction for a few hours.

This story is filled with amazing and sometimes shocking coincidences;
the purchase of the boat is just one part of this amazing and tragic story.
The day Robert and his wife, Judy, were browsing for a boat to purchase,
Robert was initially looking for a boat like his uncle had, a typical fishing
boat. However, when Judy saw the type of boats he was looking at, she
quickly objected to the design of the fishing boats. They had a two-year-old
son named Diego, and she quickly surmised that these boats were open on
the side and it would be easy for a rambunctious child to fall off into the
water. She said to Robert, "Mijo [our son] will fall off this, no way." In the
end, instead of buying a typical fishing boat, Robert ended up purchasing a
seventeen-foot Glastron ski boat. The purchase of this specific vessel over a
fishing boat would later provide the space Robert would need for the three
victims of the collapse whom he and his cousins rescued from the ocean.
The fishing boats Robert was looking at would not have had the room. Prior
to the day of the accident, they had taken the boat out only twice, and
Robert later recalled that he took a picture with his son in the boat with
the very section of the bridge that would later fall in the background of
the photo. After the accident, they never used the boat again. As Judy put
it, "That ski boat did what it was supposed to do and that was it." Robert
invited his cousins, brothers Roland and Leroy, out fishing.

Robert: Leroy and I are about the same age. I think that
if I'm not mistaken, we're a month apart. He was born in
March of '79, and I was born in April '79. Roland is his older

brother, and the three of us were inseparable. Every Friday I'd go over to Leroy and Roland's house and—and live with them until Sunday night. Basically, when we were children, I would stay with my aunt and uncle, and we literally planned our lives basically together. Leroy and I married best friends, and then we planned our boys together, and then we accomplished that, and then the girls were ready to bring another baby into the family and they wanted girls and we planned that, and we got the two girls. We were very close. Leroy, Roland, and I, back when I was sixteen, got a $5,000 loan out of 1st Valley Bank in Mission off of Conway and we opened the first Paintball Club here in the Valley. And we would drive to Corpus to go get paintballs because they still didn't sell them here back then. We wanted to do everything together and with one another. Roland was the first to find a serious girlfriend, Hope. Her younger brother, Tony, became Roland's brother-in-law after

Robert fishing below the Queen Isabella Causeway with his son days before the accident. *Courtesy of Judy Espericueta.*

high school, and then they tied the knot, which brought Tony into the group. But he wasn't a leg of the tripod you know? He just—he was more of a visitor. Somebody that we were just kind of accommodating because Roland wanted to bring one more. And so, I didn't know much about him in those days.

At the time, Leroy was living in Edinburg on a piece of property that's on 107 just near Tenth Street. And Roland is living in some apartments complex off Tenth Street right before you get to Dove. We were brought up fishing and hunting and doing all this stuff and we were always led or chaperoned by their father, my uncle. However, for whatever reason, my uncle couldn't make it, but we invited my older brother Rick and their older brother Leonard, but neither could go. So, it wound up just being the four of us, three by default because where Roland went, Leroy and I went, where Leroy went, Roland and I went.

Without a doubt, these three young men had developed a strong bond and were in a sense at the time almost inseparable. They had grown up together, shared experiences with one another and grown to love the same type of activities, such as hunting and fishing, a staple of life in the Rio Grande Valley. It was this bond that would serve them well on the night of the collapse. They worked together almost seamlessly without any actual planning or guidance to save the lives they were destined to save, in spite of the psychological trauma that would haunt them until this day.

Once Robert decided to take a fishing trip with his cousins, the next task was to convince "the law"—their wives. Robert began with his wife, Judy. Robert went to Judy as the first domino, hoping that if Judy said yes then the other wives would fall, knowing that one of them had already agreed. Judy's initial apprehension came with the fact that she would have to spend the night alone in the house with the baby, for this would be a trip to do some night fishing. As Robert stated,

Back then my wife would have to leave from Alton, Texas [which is where Robert and Judy lived at the time], and drive all the way to Weslaco (a distance of forty miles) on the nights that I would go out fishing or that I would stay out late working because we had our son, our first child. So, she would go all the way to Weslaco to spend the night with her mother. It's not so much that she didn't want us to go, it just seemed cumbersome to her because she had to load up Diego into the car seat and drive in the middle of the night. Also, Danielle, Leroy's wife, never really liked me too much. I think she was always a little jealous of mine and Leroy's bromance, you know? Consequently, anything that I did, she didn't want him to do, but he always had the ability to fight that and come along anyway.

As a result, after Judy relented, with the promise of some shopping, the phone calls began throughout the day as the other men each called one another with their plans and then, in turn, asked their wives, who in turn called one another to see if the other relented and what they were going to get out of it. As the day progressed, the dominos fell and eventually the trip received the "green light"; the young men prepared to get on the road to South Padre Island.

The trip would be challenging for Robert, because it would be the first time he took the boat out alone without his uncle guiding him at night. He had been on many trips to night fish with his uncle and had watched him maneuver the boat around the Laguna Madre (the body of water between Port Isabel and the island), the bridge and the island. He felt confident he could do the same, but there is always a bit of apprehension that comes with doing things for the first time, added to that the responsibility of having the lives of his cousins in his hands. This responsibility weighed heavily on Robert when he decided to respond to the tragic accident before him later that night.

He began their fishing trip by hooking up his new boat to his also recently purchased fire engine–red Chevy pickup, a cab and a half with flare sides that glistened in the sun. He was proud of his ability to purchase both and to be able to take his cousins out in them. Additional phone calls were made between the cousins as to who had what, tackle boxes, rods and any additional safety gear. When Robert had initially bought his boat, it did not come with any safety equipment, so he went to Academy to purchase everything they had in regard to boat safety, like floatation equipment and flares—all of which would come in handy that night.

Robert Espericueta got on the road around nine o'clock the night of the fourteenth and drove over to La Joya, then on to Edinburg to pick up Roland. Robert was unaware of Tony's presence until he pulled up to pick up Roland and saw him walking with a half smile carrying nothing and Tony, standing smaller, scrawnier, in tow carrying supplies: fishing rods, ice chest, backpack and Roland's stuff as well. Robert pulled up and rolled down the window, and Roland said, "I have to bring Tony with me, Hope says he has to come. So, he's going to be lugging everything around for us." And he looked happy to do it. Tony had just moved in with Roland because he had fallen onto some hard times, and he was not seeing eye to eye with his parents. He asked his sister Hope if he could crash at her place for a while with her and Roland. Once they were all situated in the truck, they got on the road to the island.

According to Robert,

> Everybody's quiet on the way over to South Padre Island. Back then there was no TikTok. There was no Facebook. There wasn't anything. You had a flip phone, and if you wanted to text somebody you would have to hit multiplier digits multiple times to get to a letter. And when you messed up and it was like having a heart attack or an aneurysm, like "Fuck!" and you wanted to throw the phone at the wall. So, when I say everybody is quiet, in today's day and age, the kids, the millennials, that's normal. A ride in the car with the radio is usually quiet because they're all engaged in their streams. They've been immersed in a different world. But to be quiet back when we didn't have our phones as a distraction was considered rude.

This quietness was due to everyone reflecting on their lives, both what was going on in them and the craziness of the events of the outside world. The chatter was pretty much kept at a minimum as they made their way along the expressway and then took the Highway 100 exit toward Port Isabel, which takes you through the infamous city of Los Fresnos.

> Robert: So Los Fresnos is the reason why we slow down, why every driver lowers the radio, it's where everybody is like "Calm down, let's get through Los Fresnos" and then we'll crank the back up and start partying again. I think Los Fresnos is what brought life into the truck again because Roland said from the back seat, "Hey hey, you need to slow down, we're getting through Los Fresnos," and that broke the whole thing. Everybody is on their best behavior while we travel through those few miles.

It was after they had made their way through the town and were on the next long stretch of road that Robert realized that the truck was running low on fuel. "I'm remembering that the last time the boat was in the water I didn't refuel it and so that sparked a debate." The debate focused on what they had time for and what exact order they needed to do things before they got into the water. Robert explained,

> Do we have time to pull over and get gas and load the ice chests as well as get the snacks we were going to get? Do we have enough time to do that and make it to the bait shop in time? Roland and Leroy and everybody who was hungry and had just been sitting in the truck just a few minutes too long wanted me to pull over and let them stretch their legs. I knew that the gas station wasn't going to go anywhere. It wasn't going to close and yes it was going to suck making a U-turn on Highway 100 in the middle of that little town, but the task at hand was getting bait, because without bait, what were we going to do? We didn't know anything about fishing with lures. We knew you'd get a hook, put the bait on, throw it down and you'd wait. We were novices, no, super novices.

The Quick Stop bait shop, where Robert stopped on his way to the island. *Courtesy of Joshua Moroles.*

They're practically hanging out the window yelling and screaming and clawing at the glass as I passed the gas station. I'm like "No-No, fuck you guys, I'm getting bait. We need bait and that is that. You can get your snacks there and we can get ice there and I will just need to pop a U and come back to get gas and then we'll just make this little short trip again." So that's what we did, and thank God, because I'm sure there are other methods of fishing that don't require bait or maybe I could have simply gone to Walmart to buy some I don't know. But in my mind, we had our rituals, and that's how things worked. As we were growing up, and you were on your way to fish at South Padre Island you would stop at the Quick Stop bait shop. You got what you needed there, and from there, you are on your way. Having been led through this from a child I didn't know anything different. I didn't know that there was a bait shop directly across the street because that is what my uncle's priority always was and where he always stopped. I followed him to a T. I followed what my uncle would have done, and he would have said, "No, we're getting the bait," so I went to get the bait. After all, this was my fishing trip, these were my passengers, and I invited them and really wanted to have a good time and fish.

Robert's instinct to stop at the Quick Stop would prove to be another in a long line of interesting coincidences that were part of what was destined to happen that night.

As the group approached the front doors of the Quick Stop, they saw the lights being turned off one by one inside the store, and of course, the open sign was off, all indicating that they were closed. However, the fact that the store's lights were actively being turned off let Robert know that there was still someone present inside the store. Robert then tugged on the locked door and began to knock on the glass to gain the employee's attention. Robert began to try to speak loudly through the locked glass door, begging the employee, "C'mon c'mon let us in, we just drove from La Joya [a distance of just under one hundred miles]." The employee walked up to the glass and, anticipating why someone was banging on his door, told Robert, "Nah I don't have any live bait, and we are already closed." Robert replied, "We'll take anything you have, we have cash," so the employee unlocked the door opened it, letting them in. Leroy immediately wanted to go shopping to get chips and snacks. The employee quickly shut him down, saying, "Nah, I already closed the box, so I can't sell you anything." He walked over to the refrigerator that contained the frozen bait. He pulled out a couple of plastic bags with frozen mullet, some sea lice and some other stuff and handed them to Robert.

> Robert: I could tell he was still in a hurry and a little upset. He was done with the day, I don't think it was anything personal, he just wished we hadn't pulled up. As he's ringing up on a calculator, not on like a register, it's just a table calculator, to come up with the total. I try to break the ice with the guy, and I say, "Where can we catch some fish? Where is a good place to fish?" I'm sure he hears that question all day, every day, one thousand times a day, 'cus they're a bait shop. But his mood changed, and you could see his shoulders relax, and it was almost as if he felt sorry for us. He said, "Look guys, it might get pretty choppy out there tonight." I could see he was kind of trying to see what we were in, leaning over the counter to see the boat, and then he explained, "Look why don't you just tie yourselves under the bridge? Pick a pillar, climb on it and tie yourselves up to it. Fish under the bridge tonight, and you'll catch something," and as quickly as he said it, I disregarded it.
>
> I kind of knew where I wanted to go. I had already been out there during the day a couple of times and had some successful fishing trips, but mission accomplished. I broke the ice. He was already talking to us. He wasn't at all angry. He sounded sincere and concerned, and with the transaction completed, we left. The last thing I remember was that door locking behind us as we were walking back over to the truck.

The group proceeded to gas up the vehicles and look toward crossing the Queen Isabella Causeway when they noticed what Captain Fowler (who was piloting *Brown Water V*, the barge that hit the bridge) and many others that night had noticed: the lights on the bridge were out. Indeed, there had been several reports that the lights had been out for over a week. The official Coast Guard report states, "The state did not have a preventative maintenance program or program of routine bridge lighting inspections, so the exact date any or all the navigation lights failed is not known. All

The entrance to South Padre Island at night. *Courtesy of Joshua Moroles.*

evidence leads to the conclusion that the green navigation lights were not working prior to and during the causality." The report also points out that the Coast Guard is the entity with the authority over the navigation lights.[15] The issue with the lights not only contributed to the accident but also affected where Robert would eventually take his boat out to fish.

> Robert: Coming over the causeway, we realized that the lights are out. Usually, the streetlights bounce off the shimmering water below it and it lights up the bay. The first mile is completely dark; it changes the perspective of safety you know. You just feel a little nervous. Then we get to the dock [where the KOA pier is today] and it's open, busted, broken and missing planks. It looks like it's being held together by barnacles, clams and oysters' heads. I think that's why they never change it up because they thought, "Well nobody's stupid enough to try to use it," but we were because we didn't know any better.
>
> We get there and it's early enough to get a good start; it's maybe nine o'clock or so. I put the boat on the water and turn it on, and this jet stream of water starts shooting out of the ass end of the outboard motor into the air, making a huge rooster tail fountain and I am floored, baffled. I am like, "Oh my God what is that? That's a huge leak. We can't go out like this!

The South Padre Island beach at night, showing how dark the ocean is without lighting. *Courtesy of Juan Carmona.*

What the hell!" It's the third time I've ever taken this boat out. I've never seen that happen and we're wrestling to figure out what is going on. The boat seems fine, and everything seems fine. It's just a steady stream of pressurized water making that rooster tail, and I do not want to take the boat out. I'm like no dude, something is wrong. We ran back and forth from the boat to the trailer. We finally go back to the boat and open the glove box, which contains the owner's manual.

It turns out that it's perfectly normal. Much like you'll see that rooster tail coming out of the ass end of a jet ski. Well, these motors have a setting where you can point that stream in the air, so that you can always turn your head and get a peripheral vision of it, and that always tells you that cold water is circulating and cooling your motor and coming out through this stream. Or you can point it down and wait for the alarm to go off if it gets jammed up.

I had no idea, but then as we were literally reversing the trailer into the water to reload the boat back on and call it a night, Roland, who was on the boat that was still in the water in between the dock, says, "I found it! I found it!" He starts waving the owner's manual, "It's normal you dumbasses, look motherfuckers! We've been here for an hour, goddamn it! I told you it was normal and that there was nothing wrong with your boat; it's brand new." Well once we had that settled, I went to park the trailer, ran back and we get into the water. We have just loaded three ice chests, one with bait, one with a bunch of ice for all the fish we thought we were going to catch and one with one lousy drink because we were in such a hurry, we forgot to buy all our snacks and stuff. We just went to pump gas and boom, got on the water and now we are eager to get out on the water and fish. Everybody thought the other person had loaded up the ice chest and nobody did. We were arguing with each other saying, "I saw you with cokes." "I saw you with this or that." "No man, you saw me with corn nuts and my coke, I didn't load the ice chest." Everybody was confused, we were putting out into the dark bay and my phone rang. It was my sister, Olivia.

Robert described his sister as "basically mother hen. What the mom should be doing in our family, Olivia did for us. She was the one looking out for me." Knowing he was going to be out fishing that night and viewing the weather, which mentioned that there was a small craft advisory, she decided to call and warn off Robert from fishing.

> Robert: She says, "Robert you guys need to get out of the water. There is a rip tide in the bay, and I just finished with the news and there is a small craft advisory all the boats need to be out of the bay." I'm literally on the phone with her and one hand on the steering wheel of the boat, the other hand on my ear holding my phone, and I'm looking around and the water looks fine. [That close to the shore the current's strength would not be apparent, it would not be until you are away from the shore that it would present itself.] I say, "I don't see a rip tide or current and I don't see this wind you're talking about." I'm thinking to myself, "Where is all of this?," telling my sister, "I just spent forty-five minutes convincing

South Padre Island shoreline at night. *Courtesy of Juan Carmona.*

myself that my boat was broken while looking at the water, wanting to be nothing but on it and now I'm on it and you want me to go and reload everything on the trailer that I just parked, there is no earthly way that shit is happening. We're fine, we'll call you if we need anything."

He then took his boat out, trying to get over the frustrating conversation that just happened and make his way to a relaxing evening of fishing with his cousins.

Robert: I would have normally gone toward the north, passed under the causeway and continued onto the north as far as I could go in the boat. Knowing that, I could always turn back toward the bridge and still see the very vibrant bridge lights. The bridge lights were my guide to getting me and my family back home. It is something that I learned from my uncle. I know that I docked my boat near the bridge and the boat that I had wasn't equipped with a compass. I didn't know my way around, so it was simple enough for me to understand that if the fog came in or anything happened what I needed was a landmark; the Queen Isabella Causeway lights would be my landmark, but the lights were off, so you couldn't see it. At that point, my plans to go where I had already fished prior dissolved because I was afraid to get lost in the darkness. It was then that the voice of that clerk popped into my head, "Just tie your boat under the bridge and fish," which is exactly what we did. We tied up to the exact same pillar that would later that evening be hit. By this time, everybody was just frustrated, we had worked more than we had, getting the engine working, getting in the water and finally hopping on a supporting pillar to get themselves tied down. They were ready to at long last fish.

Robert's remembrance of the conversation with the Quick Stop store clerk would be like so many events of that day, one of both fortuitousness and perhaps some divine intervention.

So now we are finally fishing, and the bait is in the water, and that sound of the tires has been with us this whole time, but when we got there, it was drowned out by the sound of the outboard motor and the frustrated banter we had amongst ourselves shouting out things like, "Pull over! Where? Where? Where? Throw the rope! Okay now jump! Climb on!" "Turn on the lights and pass me the bait." "Who has the bait? What? What? You don't have this? You don't have that?" So we're talking, and the boat is alive with shouts and movement trying to get settled in. But once the bait is in the water, the knots are tied, and everybody has come to terms with the fact that we don't have shit to drink, we're just there. Looking at the water with our fishing poles. Then all the commotion came to a crawl. Nobody was saying anything.

Then there was the sound that would haunt Robert for years, piercing through the newly found silence on the boat.

Robert: Badum Badum. Badum Badum. The sound had everyone looking up at the underside of the bridge, trying to make it in a way that signals that you are not afraid. Trying to do it in a tough but curious "Woah what is that?" We all knew what it was, and we tried to act like, why are you looking up? Ignore it, but everyone was just trying to get that "oh shit" thought out of themselves. I was thinking what everybody was thinking "Wow man, those are right above us. What would happen if one of those cars fell into the water?" Finally, Leroy was the one who said it out loud to everyone. He was one who every trip, would always have a "What if?" question or "What would you do if this" you know? They were never planned; they were always spontaneous and appropriate to whatever scenario or whatever environment we were in. He just enjoyed a good conversation, so the question didn't seem that peculiar to us. It didn't seem that out of the norm or with any kind of malicious intent. It was the sound of the tires that drew that question in all our minds, but he was just the first one to vocalize it. And he asked, "What would you do if cars just started, you know, what would you do if there was an accident up there and boom, a car just fell off and landed right next to us?" Because we are literally directly beneath it if anything falls, it's falling directly next to us, or adjacent to us. We all had our own answers; mine was nothing. Unless I recognize that person or see my mom or my son or something in that car, I'm not jumping in that dark, cold-ass water, like, no way. After everyone kicked around their own personal takes on the question. Roland's response was, "You know what man, what are the chances of that? There would have to be an eighteen-wheeler up there, would have to take out the guard rail, open the gap, cars falling, there is no way." Tony responded, "It could happen, man, the chances are probably about the same as two planes flying into the Twin Towers," and that was it, that's all it took to push us back into the moment and nobody wanted to hang out there anymore. So after only ten or fifteen minutes of being tied there, everybody was eager to get out of the way. So we did, and that's when the crash happened. That's when the rain started. That's when we saw the first set of taillights fly off from the bridge. Headlights then taillights, headlights then taillights...

Those images would forever be seared into Robert's memory, headlights then taillights. It is Robert's belief that the question posed by Leroy was not just something that arose out of the situation and Leroy's love of sparking "what if" conversations. On reflection, it was a way to subtly prepare them for the upcoming set of traumatic events. As the story progresses and other events come to light, it is a position that is hard to contradict.

Brown Water V

The following comes from the Coast Guard report on the accident:

At or near 2110 on Friday, September 14, 2001, the M/V *Brown Water V* departed Brownsville, Texas, under the control of Captain Rocky Wilson. The *Brown Water V* was pushing four loaded hopper barges ahead of it, lined up in a straight line, single file. At 2400 Captain David Fowler took the helm [while Captain Wilson went below to sleep]. The vessel successfully cleared the Long Island Swing Bridge at 0145 on September 15, and at 0200 allided [collided] almost head-on with the Queen Isabella Causeway Bridge approximately

Brownwater V. Courtesy of Joshua Moroles.

375 feet west of the channel....The allision caused two 80-foot sections of the bridge to collapse. Following the collapse, nine vehicles entered the water through the missing bridge sections, resulting in eight deaths and three injuries.

There was some damage to the alliding barge but no flooding. The coupling connecting the lead barge to the second barge was either snapped by the allision or snapped following the allusion due to the current pushing the vessel and tow to the west of the allusion point. Later that day, during the search and rescue operation, a third 80-foot section of the bridge collapsed but caused no injuries or death.

The casualty happened during the darkness of the early morning hours. Everyone on the vessel except Captain Fowler was asleep. It was determined that Captain Fowler was the best, if not only, source of information about the events leading up to the allision. Captain Fowler took the Fifth Amendment during the formal hearing. Because of this lack of testimony, it was necessary to rely on what he said about the casualty during his pre-hearing contacts with Coast Guard Investigators.[16]

As far as the crew on board, the *Brown Water V* had attached to it three licensed officers; however, at the time of the accident, only two were aboard. These two men were Captain Rocky Lee Wilson and the relief captain, David D. Fowler. At the time of the accident, all other crewmen stated they were asleep, with the deckhand Levie Old asleep on duty in the wheelhouse. The barges that they were pushing were first: NM 315, a rake barge, and three other square-end barges.

> The barges were configured under the supervision of *Brown Water V*'s captain, Rocky Wilson. In his September 17 interview with the Coast Guard, Captain Fowler indicated the horsepower and characteristics of the *Brown Water V* were adequate to handle the tow….Testimony from various witnesses at the hearing and from Captain Fowler's September 17 statement indicated loaded barges present less sail area for the wind but with more of the barge below the water surface, they are more affected by the current. With the barges loaded as heavily as they were, the current would affect the navigation, but the wind would not.[17]

According to Captain Steve Ellis, who was familiar with the route the tug would have taken, there were several factors that the captain of the barge had to contend with as he navigated his way around the shipping channel and under the causeway.

> Coming from the Port of Brownsville you need to make one turn towards Port Isabel's part of the intercoastal waterway, then make a hard right turn, to get lined up for the old swing bridge. Go through the swing bridge then make a left turn and there is only one navy buoy to turn off of. Next, the wind would come into play, and see that there were no lights to navigate the barge by, so he could not see where the opening was, where they were supposed to pass through. All they had was a spotlight to look for the entrance. As long as the barge is in the shipping channel the pressure of the water will keep it there. It's like a trench or ditch dug in the bay. It provides a little more room for the boats to pass through and if needs be you can crabwalk it in, to get it in line. The captain probably couldn't get control of the vessel due to the strong winds and rip tide pushing it

from behind. They must power up over 100% to line the boat up correctly. But it's impossible if the current is too strong and there is no way to stop when you are pushed forward by the current. There are no brakes on the boat so he could not stop.[18]

His assessment derived from his own experience on the water running the same route provides a good understanding of the forces that worked on the tug as it made its fateful journey into the bridge and disaster.

There are several comments in the Coast Guard report about these conditions. According to Vice-Commandant Michael Hugh Quinn,

> The current was a factor in this casualty but not a contributing cause. Although an exact current speed was not available for the time of the causality, it was "running hard." Scientific evidence indicates that the current speed had equaled or surpassed that of the morning of September 15 on three occasions in the previous six months. The Mariners on the witness stand testified to the methods they used to gauge the tide and current in the "S" curve prior to entering the bend before the Queen Isabella Causeway Bridge. The current was

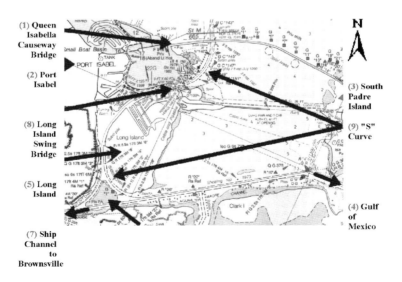

Diagram of the path of *Brownwater V*'s path through the shipping channel to the accident. *Courtesy of the United States Coast Guard accident report.*

foreseeable by a prudent mariner, and the causality was not inevitable. An accident is said to be "inevitable" not merely caused by [an] Act of God, but also when all precautions reasonably are required to have been taken, and the accident occurred notwithstanding.

However, the report's authors counter with the following statement:

We disagree with the investigator's statement that the current was not a contributing cause. A contributing cause is a condition, action, or event that when present, increases the likelihood of an accident, but that by itself does not cause the accident. Witness statements and evidence cited in sections 13 through 16 (including pages of the appendix) of the Findings of Fact consistently identify the currents at the approach to the causeway as a condition that persons operating towing vessels need to be aware of and account for properly. In addition, the final paragraph of the analysis concludes that "While the causality was caused by the failure to set up properly, mechanical failures such as a loss of steering or loss of power could result in a similar catastrophe anytime the current is running hard and despite the degree of care exercised by the vessel's operator." In other words, the existence of the cross current increases the likelihood of an accident by making the transit less forgiving of human error or mechanical failures. Therefore, we believe that the condition of the current at the time of the causality was a contributing cause.[19]

It was not just familiarity with the directions and geography of the area that would be needed that night. One must be knowledgeable of the conditions in which the vessel would be making its way, but there was a piece of evidence and the testimony provided that draw to question how much care the pilot of the vessel at the time had taken. As pointed out in the Coast Guard's report, "Coast Guard CWO Olmsted conducted a boarding of the M/V *Brown Water V* on September 15, 2001, and noted that the vessel had a copy of the local chart, Nautical 11302. Because of the difficulty, Captain Wilson had in locating the chart, and the fact that the chart was tightly folded, it was CWO Olmsted's opinion that the chart hadn't been used recently."[20] This finding leads us to the point of view that perhaps not as much care had been taken by the captain as he navigated his way through the waterways that took him to the bridge.

As part of the investigation, the Coast Guard investigated the background and experience of Captain Fowler and rendered the following to the report. On August 30, 2000, while he was at the helm of the M/V *Janice Carol* making his way through the Corpus Christi ship channel, his "inexperience with the local area and vessel, and his failure to correctly judge tidal influence directly led to the grounding of the T/B tank [tank barge] USL-148." Then again on March 7, 2001, while piloting the M/V *Golda Pickett*, the "vessel slowed to wait for westbound traffic to clear. With the speed slowed, the tide pushed the stern of the tug toward the bank. The starboard propeller touched the ground and stalled the engine. While the crew was trying to start the engine, the tug and tow drifted into the Bayou DuLarge, Houma, LA bridge."[21]

During his initial questioning, Captain Fowler stated he had been through the waterway in Brownsville perhaps fifty times, but then in an additional interview, he said he had been through the area about eight or ten times. On the other hand, according to his employer, Brown Water Marine, he had been on that route only five times. The report goes on to indicate that since the captain went on to plead his Fifth Amendment right, the investigators were not able to properly clarify his experience as a sailor in the area. All the preceding information supports the assertion that the fault may be on Fowler. Nonetheless, wherever or with whomever the fault lies, the tragedy unfolded all the same.

6

BACK ON ROBERT'S BOAT

Robert and his passengers removed themselves from the pillar and moved about 150 feet north of the bridge, which was enough distance for them to feel safe from the perceived danger that Leroy's question had placed in their psyches. Robert dropped anchor, and they tried to get back to the peace of the lapping of the waves and the gentle rocking of the boat. The length of the anchor line allowed them to drift another 20 or 30 feet north away from the bridge. Their new position took them away from what to them had been the ominous sounds of the tires hitting the various sections of the bridge and the thought of them falling on their boat and themselves. They felt safe, and silence once again fell over the Glastron. They hadn't even settled into their fishing when they heard what Robert described as the "ugliest sound I ever heard."

Robert: It was a long ongoing crashing sound. Accompanying that sound was the sound of metal like a shovel being scraped against a brick or concrete floor. A screeching ongoing sound along with boom after boom. It was so loud it seemed like it was right on us. They all tensed up and started looking around frantically trying to figure out where that sound was coming from, asking each other if they heard it, "What was that?" Someone yelled out "Look" and pointed at the causeway, and they all turned around toward the bridge to look. What they saw made them all stand up from where they

Robert pointing at the section of the bridge that collapsed. *Courtesy of Joshua Moroles.*

were. They were standing there and looking at this torrential downpour. It looked like it was just raining on this one section of the causeway. They started squinting trying to get a better view, "Is that rain? Thunder?" What was happening was that the part of the bridge which collapsed brought down so much concrete and asphalt into the water that it sent the splash so high it was taking a long time to come back down. Just seconds after they understood what they were looking at they saw the first car fly off the bridge, just completely drive off, probably didn't know the bridge had collapsed until it was too late. It cut through the rain and the taillights glowed bright red and radiated throughout all the water that was in the sky. The headlights were pointed down into the Laguna Madre, and in an instant, the car disappeared into the water.

The original huge downpour of water that they observed in awe certainly came from the huge section of concrete that slammed into the water, sending so much water up in the air that appeared to be as if there was a small cloud focusing its rain on one section of the bridge. However, the cascade of water continued, for running along the side of the causeway was a water line that sent fresh water into South Padre Island as well as an electrical line; both would hamper the rescue and recovery efforts.

The repaired pillar, the point of impact of the barge. *Courtesy of Joshua Moroles.*

As he saw more cars fall from the bridge, Robert's first instinct was to protect his family, the people on his boat. Being a captain of a boat, even the relatively small Glastron that Espericueta owned, comes with the added responsibility of the people on the boat. He might have been a young man, but he invited his cousins and a cousin-in-law, all of whom he was responsible for, and he knew he had to return them home safely. He started to turn the boat, and Roland realized that Robert's intention was to flee the scene and get to safety. So Roland moved up next to Robert and said, "Robert, we need to go over there." Robert responded excitedly, "No way, I am not going home to your mother without you guys." Robert then went back to get the boat started, and very gently, Roland placed his hands on Robert's shoulders. Then, as Robert was turning to look at Roland, Roland kissed the top of Robert's head (he had a shaved head). He said, "Robert, I know you are scared, but we need to go help. Calm down, there could be kids in the water, in those cars. We have to help." Robert felt Roland's bravery transferred to him in that kiss. He said, "You are right." He got the boat on, and they made their way to the accident site.

Robert's next action is reminiscent of the stories that have been reported regarding the events of 9/11; he picked up his phone to call his wife, Judy. As stated previously, she was staying at her mother's house while Robert went on his fishing trip. It was during the early morning hours, so Judy and

A section of the causeway being collapsed for repairs. *Courtesy of Joshua Moroles.*

the baby, whom she described as "night owls," were just getting to sleep when the phone rang. Robert came on the line with a panicked and excited voice, which made it difficult for Judy to understand him, not to mention she was groggy. She was confused by what Robert was saying. She could only recall him saying, "We are going to go see what happened and see what we can do." She just responded "OK," not knowing or understanding the seriousness of the situation and the danger Robert and his group were about to ride into. It would not be until she woke the next morning that she came to grips with what he had gotten himself into. Robert's recollection of what he was trying to explain to her was as follows:

I called Judy and said, "Babe the bridge is out. There are cars falling in the water we're going to go in and help." I didn't know it was a boat yet; I didn't know it was a barge. I said, "The bridge is out, and there are cars falling in the water we're going to go help, I love you, tell Diego I love him if anything happens to me," and click, I throw the phone back into the glove box and that was it.

Roland then attempted to call 911 to report the accident and get some help, for they were just some young guys in a fishing boat with no medical training and they needed professionals on the scene. His first call was answered by a man who could not understand what Roland was telling him and Roland grew frustrated and hung up and tried calling again. The same person answered, and he had a thick accent, so it was also hard for Roland to understand him. Roland tried to speak in Spanish in hopes that the operator would understand him, but he didn't speak Spanish. To Roland, it did not appear that he was taking the call seriously, and with the air of 9/11 on his mind, he was angry that calls like this were not being taken seriously at a time when the nation was on "high alert." Everyone else was trying to call 911 as well. Robert found himself in a similar situation, with the operator thinking it was a prank call and telling him, "You know we can trace these calls." Eventually, with the flood of phone calls, the authorities were alerted, and a response was mounted. Nonetheless, the struggle to get some help was a sign of things to come.

Robert: As soon as I agreed that we would go help, Leroy, Roland, and then everybody literally started to just throw stuff off the boat, ice chests, all the crazy stuff that we had with us in regard to the lures and baits, and the frozen fish we had just gotten from the bait shop. Because again the boat wasn't big, and we needed to make space because we were on our way to try to help. We did keep one backpack that Tony brought of extra clothes which we thought might be handy. As they were doing that, I'm still in the captain's chair. I reach into the glove box and grabbed my phone and started passing out the guys their phones because we were going to have to call our families for help. As I am cranking the boat on, I flipped my phone open and the second car comes off. Roland tells everyone that they better prepare themselves to possibly see some dead bodies.

This statement provided everyone with the context of the situation they were about to find themselves in.

We were off now keeping in mind that the anchor was still in the water, nobody had bothered to pull it in. The boat starts taking off and we're all heading towards the bridge then it gets to the point where we pass the anchor. We kept going and eventually, we passed far enough to where the rope started dragging the anchor it bites into the ground sending all of us flying and crashing into one another because it was tied to the bowl of the boat. It flipped my boat around and it just twisted us and mangled us within the confinements of the small boat I was wearing like this wrist wire thing that attaches to the key so when I came out of my chair the engine shut off, we had to compose ourselves, and in my mind, never in a million years, I would've thought that it was the anchor. In my mind, for whatever reason, I thought it was somebody that shot us, you know, something. I thought we were under attack and that's when Roland started yelling "It's the anchor! It's the anchor!" We got it up, put my key back in and turned on the boat as we were collecting ourselves the third, then the fourth car fell in and we stopped, looked and yelled. Then my boat turned on and by the time we got there the last two cars were flying in right over us at that point, we began to spark the flares.

As we were looking up helplessly from the boat below the bridge all I would hear is the engines revving, illustrating for me and in my mind that the person on their way down into La Laguna Madre was slamming in a desperate last resort on the pedals, both the gas and the brakes. Because you could see the lights just flare, they looked like dragons about to just blow fire out. Because on the way down they would just illuminate red. Then you'd hear the roar of the engine. We're looking at it, and we're yelling, and it was almost as if everything, every time a car flew off the bridge was a symphony of yelling and of screeching of the brakes and the engines revving.

That moment had its own pulse; I don't know how to explain it. I panicked. I didn't want to get anywhere near there; my first fear was that something would happen to one of us and then I would return to my aunt and uncle without one of their sons. Keep in mind that for the first five to ten minutes, I was utterly convinced that we were under attack by terrorists. Profoundly convinced. Big rocks and chunks and slabs would fall in random orders and patterns and slap the water, and they would sound like gunshots. The Twin Towers have just fallen, and now I'm looking at cars that fall eighty-seven feet off the top of the bridge into the waters. I'm also looking at a section of a bridge that I just an hour prior drove over and never would imagine anything could take it out and now she's hemorrhaging cars.

So we get there, and now we see the barge and all the people on board were panicking and they were trying to signal oncoming traffic with their big spotlight, and they start yelling at us get out of the way you know, and warning us so immediately we realize that they are not terrorists attacking because everybody on my boat's first thought was "we're under attack." They are not trying to harm us. They're doing the exact opposite; they are trying to get us out of harm's way. Telling us to get out of the way, more cars are coming. We're yelling back at them trying to figure out what exactly happened. It's chaos, with those on the boat's deck arguing amongst themselves as well. Eventually, they disappear below. We go on our way to try to help who we could.

Once they were under the bridge, they began to light their flares and swing them around in the air in a desperate attempt to warn those above that the bridge was out.

Robert: The wind was blowing, not one of us had ever used a flare before and we did not know as they were burning, they are melting, rapidly like a candle. What was melting was the consistency of lava and we did not realize that it was dripping all over us. [This could be due to the adrenaline that was no doubt pouring through their bodies.]

Eventually, somebody above us saw our flares, pulled over to the side of the road, and peeked over the bridge down to us. Completely oblivious that the bridge was out. They were trying to see if we needed help, and we yelled, "The bridge! The bridge! The bridge!" and he started using the rail, the concrete rail as a guide and ran to where we were pointing and the last thing we heard was, "Oh my god! Oh my god! Oh my god!" and he disappeared. It was because of that person that traffic finally stopped.

I just remember seeing him running right on the shoulder lane, holding onto the barrier that would keep him from falling off the bridge. One hand placing it over the barrier one hand over the other. We could see him and then suddenly, he saw the barge and the gaping hole in the bridge. I think he either parked his car in a way it blocked the road, or he just began to wave at cars, stopping them. He ultimately saved countless lives. I never heard from him or of him, or—or never heard anybody say, "Oh that was me," but I'm fully aware that in the spot we were in if you were on the bridge, we were so close to the pillars that we were invisible to the vehicles. It was when we ventured north as we were circling looking for survivors with the flares and our spotlight to try to gain the attention of the drivers—that's when the guy saw us and ultimately stopped everybody.

7
GUSTAVO MORALES

THE LAST CAR IN THE WATER

That Friday night, Gustavo Morales was working as a restaurant manager at Señor Donkeys on the island. It being a typical Friday night, he was coming to the end of a busy shift. He completed his final duties for the night, ensuring the restaurant was clean and ready for the next day. He then got into his car to head home for the night. At the time of the accident, Gustavo's wife was six and a half months pregnant, and as per usual, he picked up his phone to call his wife and let her know he was on his way home, telling her, "I will see you in about twenty or thirty minutes." He hung up and began his drive across the bridge, to the mainland and home. He

Gustavo Morales looking out into the bay where the accident happened. *Courtesy of Joshua Moroles.*

noticed the clock on his truck read 1:43 a.m. as he pulled out of the parking lot to head toward the causeway. Making his way on the causeway, he did notice some lights in the bay. The lights would turn out to be the spotlights that the barge was using in a desperate attempt to let people know the bridge was out by pointing them straight up into the sky where the collapse had occurred. However, Morales thought it was people out night fishing and did not know the danger that lay ahead of him.

According to Gustavo, he kept driving, and "thirty seconds later I was flying." On the way down, he slammed on the brakes out of sheer instinct and panic. He believes it took him about two seconds to hit the water, a fall of about eighty feet. The fall felt like a roller coaster, and on his way, he could see the water bursting from the broken water pipe and cascading like a waterfall into the ocean. The second he hit the water, he started to panic and attempted to kick and punch the window in a vain attempt to break it open so that he could escape. He thought, "God please don't let me die like this, not now." Within moments, the car began filling with water; it started coming in from where the pedals were and into the rest of the car. His initial panic was inexplicably overcome by a real moment of calm, and he was able to think clearly about his situation. At that moment, he realized two things: one was that he was still strapped into his seatbelt and could not extricate himself until he removed it, and second, the truck had manual windows so he could simply roll them down and swim to the surface to safety. Morales did not have far to swim to get to the surface because each of the cars had landed on top of the other, and his being the last vehicle meant that he was closer to the surface of the water. When he got to the surface, he could see the gap in the bridge where it had collapsed. He realized he did not go straight up but had gone off to one side (probably because of the strong current); his plan was to try to swim to one of the pillars, climb up and await rescue. Throughout the entirety of his fall, his escape and his swim to the surface, Gustavo's family was on his mind; they were what drove him to survive and be there for them, to take care of them.

He was in a lot of pain but fortunately had suffered only some torn ligaments, scratches and bruises. He felt most of the pain in his leg and took a moment to float on the surface to gather himself for a swim to safety. Then he heard another survivor, Brigette Goza, yelling, and they began to yell at each other in the dark so that they knew that they were not alone. As he floated in the water, he could smell a strong odor of gas and saw a lot of debris in the water, which was what he was holding onto when Robert found him.[22]

8

BACK ON THE BOAT

Robert: When we got to the place where all the cars were falling, piling on top of each other, there were still parts of the concrete and the asphalt from the bridge falling sporadically into the water. We would be hearing these booms as another big chunk would fall and crash into the water.

It was immediately relevant to them that the bridge was not stable. The big ten-inch water main line that takes fresh water into the island was severed and spewing water in a cascade over the crash site, creating a curtain of water falling eighty-seven feet. Consequently, every time they moved into the collapse site, the water hit their boat, causing it to shake violently, and pushed them around. The last vehicle to come off the bridge (Gustavo's truck) flew right over the nose of their boat and into the water. It was noisy and chaotic on the boat—Robert told everyone to "Shut up! We are not going to hear people if they are yelling for help because we are making too much noise!" Once they understood, they all quieted up and took a deep breath and listened, and they heard a cry from behind them. It was Goza.

The noise took Robert and his flashlight/spotlight to the vicinity of her calls for help, and they finally came upon her arm waving from the water.

Robert: Seeing her hand was the first small relief I felt from the time the bridge collapsed till that moment. It was as if we had been holding our breaths underwater until that moment. As soon as I saw her, I felt like I could breathe. I felt relief that somebody had survived. As soon as they got next to her she practically helped herself onto the boat. We offered her our hands and she just pulled herself onto the boat. They finally had a feeling of usefulness. It had been robbed of us with every car that fell off and they could do nothing but watch. Finding her gave them the energy and the motivation to keep on and continue to look.

A brief note on Robert and his compatriots' search for victims in the water: Robert describes the struggle of using his handheld spotlight in a moving boat as sitting in a dark room with a flashlight and trying to find a single ant. For not only is the ocean vast and that night not well lit, but when he heard someone's cry for help and he turned the boat toward that direction, he also had to deal with the fact that the front of the boat rose as he added speed, causing him to completely lose sight of what he was heading for. At times he had to stop and look again and redirect. Their search was also hampered by all the debris floating in the water: clothes, papers and other items from the various vehicles in the water that had floated out from broken windows, trunks and car doors.

Another aspect of the rescue effort that one must keep in mind as the rest of the tale unfolds is the fact that the water line was broken by the collapse, and the power line that was torn apart but still had power running through it was dangling alongside the cascading waterfall created by the broken water pipe. This created a highly dangerous situation for anyone who was attempting to get inside the area of the collapse. There was this constant swinging of the live wire through the falling water, causing a flashing of light and the snapping sound of the wire as it set off sparks when it hit the water. Another disturbing sound of the night was the constant smashing and crashing of pieces of concrete that continued to fall from the bridge. The sound created by these concrete pieces was almost like small explosions all around the bridge. Everyone, including Robert, who heard it thought it could be explosions from a possible terrorist attack, and it kept his and the others' anxiety at extreme levels.

Brie was hysterical when she got onto the boat—she was thoroughly convinced that she had somehow caused the accident. To Robert, it appeared as though she was reliving the accident in her head over and over because she went from periods of calm to outright hysterics. At one point, she jumped back into the water to retrieve her purse and came back up with it. Once they finally had her calm in the boat, they explained to her that they had to keep searching for other survivors. They wrapped her in T-shirts and whatever else they had on hand, and then Roland said to everyone, "Be quiet," so that they could see if there was someone else that they could save.

They all became quiet, and then they heard Gustavo's cries for help. However, the boat motor was still going, and they could not exactly hear where his cries were coming from. So Roland reached over and turned off the motor. Right after that, they heard him clearly—he was just a few yards away. As they made their way to Gustavo and were clearing an area for him to get into the boat, someone yelled, "Look there is somebody over there!" They all looked and saw a woman in waist-deep water waving her hands at them. She was in a soaking-wet white dress bobbing up and down and rapidly drifting away from them. Robert could not keep the spotlight on her and at the same time continued to navigate his boat to pick up Gustavo. Gustavo gave them a thumbs-up that he was OK; they then tossed him a floatation device so that they could continue to look for the woman.

The lady appeared to be drifting away from them quite rapidly, so Robert gunned the engine and headed in her direction. As he was attempting to make his way to her, he began to think of giving her a floatation device while he tried to figure out how to get and fit everyone on board. As he sped toward her, the boat periodically rose and he lost her; just as the boat came back down, he could see her. Moments before he arrived, she seemed to melt back into the water. Everyone went to the edges of the boat with their flashlights looking for her, and that's when they saw a young man floating face down in the water. This was Rene Mata.

Roland and Leroy, without uttering a word, immediately jumped into the water to get to him. Robert quickly shut off his boat because he was afraid that he might run someone over. Before they flipped the man in the water over, they thought he was dead, but once they flipped him, he let out a huge cry. The first word out of his mouth was "Robin." They struggled to get him on the boat; he was soaked and unconscious, and they had to use all their strength to get him out of the water and onto the boat. When they finally pulled him onto the boat, he heard Brigette's voice and said, "Is that Robin?" Yeah, yeah," Roland responded. At that point he did not know Brigette's name. As they laid Rene down, he called out to her, "Robin, Robin." She said, "My name is Brigette." He responded, "Where is Robin?" Roland said, "We are looking for her," but Rene pushed them away. "No leave me alone, look for Robin."[23] Robin was his girlfriend; she had been in his vehicle at the time of the accident. Rene was in the Valley from Houston to attend his mother's funeral; he had taken Robin out on his last week in the Valley. Sadly, she was later recovered in the back seat of the car, probably sent flying back by the impact of the fall, which is also why Rene was so injured and in pain. He had a gash from his eyebrow to the back of his ear. It was deep and open; you could almost see the brain. Tony took off his shirt and put it over the wound.[24]

They then believed that the woman they saw before they found him was Robin, so they started to look and went in circles searching and searching for her everywhere. They could not find her, and off in the distance, they could hear Gustavo's cries. He too was drifting away, so they decided to abandon their search and go get him into the boat. Robert had to leave Gustavo for a moment to make a big circle with his boat to come around and get him because of the strong rip current. Gustavo yelled at him, "Hey where are you going?" Robert made his way back toward him so they could get him on the boat. Roland and Robert dove in, but they could not swim down because of their life jackets. They took off their jackets and thought that since their anchor line was broken, they could tie their ankles to the rope and swim, but the current was too strong. Robert said, "If you jumped in the water you had to be careful not to be carried away." When they finally got Gustavo on the boat, he immediately asked for a phone and called his parents, but they did not answer. He called two or more times with no answer. His dad later told him it was after 2:00 a.m. and he saw a weird number, so he did not answer, thinking it was drunk kids. Then he called his wife, who answered, and he told her what had happened. She was wondering how it had happened, and he still wasn't sure, but he was OK. He told her not to worry but asked her to go to his parents' house and let them know what had happened. In the boat, because of the pain in his leg, Gustavo was lying stretched out on the floor staring up into the night sky. Everyone was asking him what had happened to his clothes, but he was not answering—his mind was somewhere else, probably in shock. Tony Salinas described the sight of Gustavo's shredded shirt as looking like he had been attacked by horror movie icon Freddy Krueger.[25]

Now they had all three survivors in the boat, they were composing themselves after all that had just transpired. Then they were startled by a loud bullhorn being blown by an approaching Coast Guard vessel, USCGC *Mallet* WLIC75304. Robert pleaded with them, asking for

Coast Guard construction vessel, similar to the one that responded to the accident. *Courtesy of Joshua Moroles.*

help, and described the situation. The response from one of the men on board was, "We don't even have a flashlight, what do you want us to do? Everything is in the water already." The Coast Guardsmen started passing around cigarettes, and one of them asked around, "Anyone got a lighter?" Then the same person called down to Robert's boat, "Does anyone have a lighter?"

> Robert: You know they were just real crass to be asking us for a lighter to light the cigarettes while at the same time, they are looking down seeing our boat full of injured people, bleeding and crying in pain. Finally, someone comes out and says, "No man you guys got to go under the bridge and go to that other Coast Guard vessel over there on the other side of the bridge. They're helping, they'll help you out." Just as callous as if we were asking for directions or something. We did that, but as soon as Brigette realized that they were going to have to cross under the bridge again, she started screaming, "Don't take me there! Keep me away from there!" She was hysterical. In fact, anytime we got near the causeway she would go into hysterics.

In a subsequent interview by Robert and Joshua, some light was shed on the actions of the Coast Guardsmen aboard the *Mallet*. Jeff Lester, E-5 food service specialist, who was on board the *Mallet* at the time of the accident, stated:

> It's a construction boat, not built for search and rescue, it's a seventy-five-foot tugboat cabled to an eighty-four-foot barge. It has a big engine, and it's not the kind of boat that you can just turn on and get underway. We felt very helpless. They could all see what was happening; everyone was exhausted from clearing the deck. They were moving slowly towards the bridge at about six knots, basically walking towards the bridge. They did not have divers and really could not do anything other than observe. There was a good chance that since it was so close after 9/11 that the senior chief probably told the captain to proceed with caution and not put the crew in any danger, because at that time no one knew what was really going on. He is certain that everyone was thinking it was a terrorist attack.

One incident that really stood out in his memory and scarred him was the fact that he witnessed a woman being pulled out of the back of a Mustang.

> She looked really busted up and they could tell she had really fought to try to get herself out. He went and took a video interview of the rescuer and asked him what he thought happened because the windows looked pinkish. He said she survived the initial impact and made her way to the back window to try and get herself out and during the struggle she probably ingested water and threw it up, repeatedly, and what was on the window was stomach contents. Her hands were badly damaged from her struggle to bust through the window.

Tragically, the woman he saw being pulled from the Mustang was Robin, whom Rene had been calling out for from the moment they pulled him from the water. Additionally, as Lester stated, the fear of the unknown, as to whether the incident was a terrorist attack, loomed large in the decisions made that night by everyone involved.

Being sent back under the bridge, Robert had one more goal. There was still one more person they wanted to rescue: Gaspar Hinojosa. Robert saw Gaspar's car fall. He heard the screeching of the brakes. Gaspar then put his foot on the gas, in an attempt to jump across the broken piece of the bridge. Had he not braked first, he might have had more momentum when he flew off. He hit the pillar and then slid down to the concrete base/platform.

> Robert: What I remember the most was the yells. I could hear him screaming "Saca me!" (Get me out). His screams would echo through the underbelly of the bridge. He was probably screaming to let people know he was alive.

9

GASPAR HINOJOSA

According to Gaspar Hinojosa's son Gaspar Hinojosa II, in the past, his father was an owner of several Starz and Sonic restaurants in the Rio Grande Valley. He was responsible for the invention of the limeade and the cherry limeade drinks that they make there; he created them and gave them to the company. He was also responsible for the cream slush. His father had at one time been a very influential businessman. However, when Gaspar II was approximately ten or eleven years old, his parents got divorced. In order not to lose the stores in the divorce, he signed the stores over to a business partner, who refused to give them back. This left him with nothing, and he had to attempt to start at the bottom and work his way back up. He tried to apply for various jobs, but didn't get hired because he was too qualified—potential employers feared that with his experience he might eventually take over their position.

When Gaspar II was nineteen years old, his dad really hit rock bottom and he and his brother kept trying to reach out to him because was going through some deep depression. This led to them reconciling just three months before the accident. One day Gaspar Sr. was calling around trying to get someone to take him for a drink, and both Gaspar II's sister and brother said no. By the time he finally got around to calling his son Gaspar, Gaspar (the son) had found religion, and when his dad called to ask him to take him for a drink, they argued for a bit but then eventually compromised. The agreement was, they would go out, but he could only be there until a certain time and after that, he would do whatever his son wanted. His father agreed, which was the first time ever Gaspar II had ever talked like that to his father, putting his foot down with him. Father and son went to a little bar; Gaspar Sr. was kind of flirting with the women who were there. Then Gaspar II told his dad that his time was up, and he responded, "All right, let's do whatever you want to do."

At the time, Gaspar II and his friends worked at a local restaurant, and they had a little Christian club where you could hang out and socialize, play pool and just hang out. It was called "J.C.'s Cafe." He took his dad over there, and at that point, none of his friends knew his background, his history or his family. They assumed that his dad was a strong Christian man. He got there, sat his dad down and went to the cook and told him that his dad had been drinking and needed something to eat, something to soak up all the alcohol. The cook responded with a quizzical "OK." Within a few minutes of getting their food, they were "munching out," and friends were stopping by and saying hi and introducing themselves to Gaspar's father. When they said "Praise God" and different religious things, a language that he was not familiar with, he just responded with "All right" and "OK." Then Gaspar II told his dad that he wanted him to come to church with him. He responded, "All right, all right son."

Gaspar II took his father to a small, intimate church service; the worship music was quiet, very peaceful and beautiful. After a little time being there, he caught him trying to sing along with the music and hymns. He began to start singing with him, and he caught him trying to open up and begin to break down. The service really hit him. He turned to his father and asked him, "Are you OK?" and he said, "I never thought my son would teach me how to live." It took him aback, and then they hugged each other; it was a very emotional and amazing moment. This all happened three months prior to the accident. He faced his demons, quit drinking, reached out to friends and family and apologized for his past behaviors. He was fifty-two years old and living in Alamo, Texas, at the time. He was offered a job managing a Whataburger on South Padre Island because of his previous experience and was coming home from work the night he fell from the causeway.[26]

10

J.P. MONTOYA (EMT/ FIREFIGHTER)

At the time of the accident, J.P. Montoya's primary job was with the Brownsville Fire Department and his second job was working for Port Isabel Emergency Medical Service (EMS). Brownsville did not pay well, so he took the second job. He had previously worked with the director of Port Isabel EMS, and he needed extra income, so the director offered J.P. some hours at his department. J.P. always carried his radio with him, and in the middle of the night, chatter came over the radio that the bridge had collapsed and we might be under attack. He told his partner they should go check it out.

They arrived and made their way to the Dolphin Watch Pier. They stood there looking at the crazy scene around the bridge collapse, trying to figure out how to get over to help in the rescue. The captain of the Dolphin Watch vessel saw them and told them to get their gear and load it onto the boat and he would take them out. They did, even though they were still under the impression that they were under attack. J.P. radioed Brownsville and San Benito to send their dive teams and ambulances, and then they took off into the bay and toward the site of the accident. As they were about to leave, Los Fresnos EMS showed up and joined them on the boat. When they approached, they could see the car stuck on the pillar; the engine had popped out of it and landed next to it. There were four rescuers who would now attempt to affect this most unusual and dangerous rescue. Just being able to make their way onto the pylon was a dangerous and difficult act. To jump onto the pylon, they had to time the jump with the waves, which were pushing them up and down, toward and away from the pillar. They had to wait until the height of the wave was sufficient to make the jump safely onto the concrete pillar. They then also had to use the same method to toss equipment over to those who were on the pylon first to have what they needed.

It was a very limited amount of space that they would be working in. They were all crammed around the pillar and the vehicle. J.P.'s partner David Lopez glanced inside the vehicle, saw that there was a man stuck inside and called everyone over to see what they could do. Montoya was the smallest one in the group, and it was decided that he would be the one to try to get inside the vehicle and attempt to rescue the victim. Montoya described the situation, stating, "This was the kind of rescue/removal you don't train for." First, the car was not stable; it was moving and still had the very real possibility of falling over and into the ocean. David got some rope to tie it up with, but even that did not guarantee that the car would not fall, especially as they introduced a rescuer into the car itself and pulled the victim out. All of this could displace the car's weight and send it over.

They began by taking off the windshield and gaining a better understanding of how to best approach the victim and extricate him. As J.P. made his way into the vehicle, he took with him a cervical (c) collar. A c collar is an immobilization device that keeps the spine from moving around. The first five cervical vertebrae control your breathing, blood pressure, temperature and more—all your vital functions—and as a paramedic, you are trained to always assume there might be a c-spine fracture to be on the safe side. This is also why medical professionals implore people not to move those who have been involved in an accident. It is one of the most common injuries in a traumatic accident, especially car accidents in which a person's neck can be hyperextended back and forth over the headrest of the car seat. As J.P. glanced around the car, it was so damaged that he could not even recognize it as the inside of a vehicle. By the time J.P. got in the car, Gaspar Hinojosa could no longer speak. (He had been hollering ever since he hit the pillar, and it was what caught those on Robert's boat's attention.) J.P. observed that Gaspar's chest was moving paradoxically (one side going up while the other side was down, then vice versa). This is known as a "flail chest" and is indicative of multiple rib fractures. Gaspar came to life a bit as he noticed the activity in and around his vehicle and asked if he was even alive. David said yes, and then Gaspar gave a thumbs-up.

Even though they really could not talk and communicate with each other, J.P. did his best to reassure and comfort Gaspar by talking to him, saying, "We are going to get you out of this." J.P. quickly glanced around the remains of the car and assessed the situation. He estimated that the victim was approximately six feet tall and weighed around 260 to 270 pounds, so it was not going to be easy to get him out. He thought about getting the jaws of life, but that would take too long. This was followed by his initial assessment of the victim to ascertain how injured he was. The steering column was broken off and lying off to the side; he could grab the whole steering column and move it away. The seat had been broken to the point that Gaspar was almost lying flat in the back seat. His head was lying on the backseat headrest. The passenger side was almost completely gone. The other rescue workers had managed to get the passenger door pushed to the front to give them access to the inside of the car. They managed to get a backboard in, to immobilize the victim's spine. Gaspar's legs were stuck in the front of the car. The right leg was easier to get out than the left, which was stuck. He was making muffled screams; something was wrong with his jaw, and he could not speak. His left leg was broken into many pieces and stuck under the dashboard. J.P. warned his patient, "I know you are in a lot of pain, but I am going to have to cause you some more pain to get your leg out of here." Gaspar gave him a thumbs-up in response. J.P. moved down toward his leg, pulled as hard as he could and felt it snap. He could hear Gaspar make some muffled screams, but he managed to get the leg free. He went back up to Gaspar's head to talk to him. J.P. apologized for what he had to do to free him and the further pain he had caused. He told him, "I am sorry, but I had to get you out."

The rescuers outside the car took a few minutes trying to decide exactly how they were going to coordinate the patient out from the car and negotiate from there out onto the boat. As J.P. waited for them, he looked down into the water and could see that the lights from the cars in the water were still on, giving a strange reddish glow to the water just below them. He also realized that there were probably still people down there. As he pondered the poor victims underwater, David yelled into the car, "If you go into the water we will get you out." It had not been uttered out loud, but it was something all the rescuers knew: the car was unstable in its position and could go over at any time. J.P. looked directly into Gaspar's face and told him, "If you feel a rush of water, hold your breath. We are both going in and we are both coming out." He gave another thumbs-up.

It was difficult to get him on the backboard because he was so broken up; his legs would dangle off to one side and the other. J.P. asked for someone to grab Gaspar's pant legs. He had to get underneath him to get the c-collar and backboard on, and Gaspar was a big guy; J.P. struggled to do it all by himself. He got to the point where his muscles were on fire and he thought he was going to fall into the water. Someone grabbed the victim by the belt, giving J.P. a small break to regain his strength. He regrouped and got back to work, and with everyone's help—including Hinojosa, who managed to grab hold of the side of the car with his one good arm and assist—they were finally able to get Gaspar out of the car.

By the time they were out of the car, they found a Coast Guard vessel alongside the Dolphin Watch boat. Getting him onto the boat was difficult, because once again they had to time what they were doing with the waves and they had to do it quickly because he was so heavy. The medics had already started IV lines so they could give him some fluids and have openings to administer more medications if needed. This was easily done because he was not moving very much anymore. They got him to the bayside and into an ambulance; they told the EMTs that he was in bad shape, and J.P. told the medic, "Hey man, take care of this guy." Sadly, Gaspar Hinojosa did not make it. J.P. said, "It was a real bummer. The time from when we got him out of the vehicle until we got to the bayside was thirty to forty minutes, way too long. If you are still on the scene by the time reporters show up, you have been there way too long, and there were already reporters there, lights, cameras and microphones."[27]

11

BACK ON THE BOAT

Robert and his companions, including the recently rescued, headed back under the causeway to the other Coast Guard ship. On the way, they tried to get to the car that was stuck on the pillar because they could hear the occupant yelling and knew he was still alive, but boats from different authorities were blocking anyone from getting close.

Robert: Authorities were yelling, screaming, using foul language. They would use their boats to try to move us away by coming alongside and pushing their boat into ours. They would act like they were getting close to talk to us and then start to push us away. One example is a state trooper who approached us on one of their boats and called us over, motioning to us as though he wanted to tell them something. As we got close to each other he pushed his boat against mine and revved his engine and pushed us away quite harshly... yelling, "You need to get away" from a bullhorn. He did [not] know we had injured people on the boat or that we were the first rescuers. It was an all-out brawl; it was chaotic. All of which were a result of the fear that they were all experiencing. When we looked past the boats along the way, we felt a brief sense of joy when rescue workers finally made it to the car and someone was finally going to help him.

As they continued their way under their bridge, they came across a large boat that had two Port Isabel firefighters dressed in scuba gear. The operator of the boat they were on was refusing to get any closer to the site of the accident. For there was still the live wire swinging in the air along with the gushing water, and pieces of the bridge were occasionally crashing down into the water. Robert could see in their faces the rescue personnel were angry and desperate to get to the accident site. They could see Robert's boat and how he was maneuvering more easily in the water and near the accident scene and called out to him and asked him if he could take them to the accident site. Robert said he would and approached their vessel, and they jumped onto Robert's boat. They had to land on the bow of the ship, because the boat was divided into three parts: the front, middle and back. In the back was Rene, lying across a padded bench. Seated on the floor in front of him were Brigette and Gustavo. In the middle, seated in the two captain's chairs, were Robert and Leroy, with Tony just behind Robert. Finally, Roland was in the front keeping an eye out for them. It was on either side of him that the divers found any space on the crowded boat. They asked if he and his companions had seen a red truck go into the water, and they said yes. They asked because this was the vehicle that their chief, Bob Harris, was known to drive.

Bob Harris was chief of the Port Isabel Fire Department and before the accident was working security at Louie's Backyard, a popular waterfront restaurant and bar on the island. However, as many first responders and as his responsibility as chief dictated, he was wearing his radio, and he overheard that there was an accident on the bridge. He immediately dropped what he was doing, got in his truck and raced to the bridge to help. Sadly, he, like the others who went into the water, could not see the gap in the bridge, nor did he understand the nature of the accident. In fact, the reason that Robert and his cousins were in the water for so long without any assistance is that emergency responders thought that the accident was on the bridge, not the bridge itself. Consequently, there was a lot of wasted time as rescuers made their way onto the bridge from both sides and realized that the bridge was out and they could do nothing from above, minus blocking the road. They would then have to make their way back off the bridge, search for rescue boats and trucks to hitch them up and take them to the docks and launch them into the water. They were joined by different ship captains who volunteered to assist in the rescue.

As Robert approached the accident site, he and his companions were once again confronted by authorities who yelled at them, "Where are you going!" "You can't go near there!" Department of Public Safety (DPS) boats again attempted to block their path, but one of the firefighters told him, "Pass them! Go around them!"

> Robert: They were eager to get into the water because someone they loved and respected, spent countless nights in the firehouse [with,] was in the water. They dove in, and after eight to ten minutes they came back up and stated sadly, "This is a recovery, not a rescue." When he removed his goggles, we could see how broken up he was with his discovery.

Meanwhile, as the diver was in the water, a DPS boat arrived and was arguing with Robert, telling him "You have to get away," blaring their horns. He attempted to explain that he was waiting for the firefighters to come up from the water. As they were speaking to each other, the boats were drifting with the current, which was still quite strong, and they were moving away from where the divers went in. As a result, while the conversations were occurring, Robert kept having to steer back to where the divers were. The current was something all those in the water would have to deal with as they went from one boat to another or into the water and back. Once the divers made their way onto the boat, one of them asked Robert if he had any problems placing a dead body in the boat. Robert responded that he did not mind, but it did not happen. Eventually, the firefighters spoke with the DPS, and things calmed down. They boarded the DPS boat and dismissed Robert and company.

> Robert: There was no structure to the rescue, no visible plan of what to do if the bridge collapsed. It was just a cluster of boats everywhere, lights all over the water. Rescue boats, personal boats, onlookers.

They then finally made their way under the causeway and to the south side of the bridge, which was where the other Coast Guard vessel was waiting for them, and it came alongside the boat. It was a difficult feat, since both crafts were having to deal with the incredibly strong current flowing all around. Once they were able to affect this maneuver, the men on the Coast Guard vessel lowered a gurney down to Robert's boat.

> Robert: Someone hollered down instructions on how to secure Rene (he was the most injured of all the victims, so

he was first to be attended to) to the stretcher as they were looking down from the safety of their large vessel down to my little vessel that is just shocked full of blood and chaos, pain and fear. We strapped him in, and they told us, "Okay now feed him up to us." We really struggled because we were basically lifting dead weight, while we were dealing with a boat that is being shaken and almost capsizing as we all migrate to one side of the boat to lift him up. It was chaotic, to say the least, and with all that motion and commotion on the boat, it almost capsized the boat. Brigette and Gustavo had become very eager to get off the boat. Because it seemed very unstable, they started to try to climb up onto the Coast Guard ship.

As they began to try to make their way onto the ship, the captain of that vessel comes out and starts violently and viciously barking at us saying, "Nah! We're not a medical vessel. Those people need medical attention." He was yelling at everyone just as they had finally placed Rene onto their boat. After the captain yelled at us and the crew, they began to lower him back to us and feed him back onto my boat. This was followed by them kicking Brigette and Gustavo off their boat and sending them back down to mine. At this point, one of the Coast Guardsmen, who I only know his first name was Chris, sees my fear and anxiety over what's happening and decides to abandon his boat and jump onto mine. His captain tells him, "Take him to the Coast Guard station." We were literally a four-and-a-half to five-minute boat ride away from where the EMS people had set up a command station on the Port Isabel side for the accident, and he had just sent us clear across the other way to the island.

Chris got on the boat and immediately took control of the situation; he took the wheel with one hand and glanced around, observing the scene, as he made his way to the Coast Guard station. Robert was now able to move around the boat to see what he could do to help the victims. The water became super choppy on the way over to the station, and with every bounce of the boat, Rene, Gustavo and Brigette cried out from the pain of their injuries. The waves slapped hard against the boat. Robert made his way over to Rene and asked him if he needed to call someone for him. He looked up at Robert and gave him a number, which Robert immediately dialed. It began to ring, and he told Rene that it was ringing. A woman answered the phone, and Robert frantically began to explain to her what was happening. She immediately began trying to calm him down. "*Tranquilo. No te mortifiques.*

Things are going to be OK, just calm down." Then she hung up the phone. Robert just stared at the phone and thought that she may have been half asleep and didn't really realize that she was answering the phone. He told Rene that he just called the number and had spoken to his mom, and she said to be calm, everything is going to be OK. Rene looked back at him. By this point, he had an ice pack on his face, and he looked around it to see Robert and told him, "No, call again." He called again, and the same lady answered and repeated, "Everything is OK. You are safe now." Robert replied, once again telling her, "Ma'am your son was in a car accident, and he fell off the bridge." She said, "Just be calm, everything is OK," and hung up again. Robert told Rene what had happened on the phone, and he could see him become angry and frustrated trying to sit up, but he couldn't with his injuries. Exasperated, Rene said, "You are calling the wrong number." By that time, they were at the Coast Guard station and had begun to dock, so no more calls were placed at the time.

> Robert: When we get there Chris jumps off the boat and hauls ass around the corner and just disappears. We stayed on the boat and began to unload for a second time. We got Rene and everybody off onto the dock and all the while we are smack-dab in the center of the largest swarm of mosquitoes I've ever seen in my life. You could almost taste them. There was a pungent odor all around the dock, and with every swat of your hand in the open air, you could feel them crashing up against your palm. There were millions of them. We stayed behind waiting for Chris, protecting one another. We are also swatting and fanning away mosquitoes from Rene's face, because he's tied to a gurney, trying to make sure that he's not getting bitten.

The group placed Rene on a nearby park bench. Gustavo stood nearby, and Brigette began to pace around in circles.

> Robert: In the corner of my eye I see Chris coming back around walking away from the Coast Guard station, looking dejected, and he just looks at me, and he says, "There's nobody here. There's an ambulance in the back but there is nobody tending it. Even if we get into it, we can't cross the bridge and the hospitals aren't on the island." And he

points way past me towards Port Isabel and says, "We should have gone over there" he said. We don't have any time to be disappointed about time being wasted. The mosquitoes are literally chasing us away. We load everybody up into the boat and we rapidly reverse out of that dock and make our way across the bay to Port Isabel.

As they were making their way back across the bay, Robert went back to check on Rene, and once again Rene asked him, "Can you call my father?" Robert pulled out his phone and asked for the number, in hopes that he would give him a different number than the one he had before. However, it was the same number, and he could see on his call log that he had already typed that number in but continued to dial. This time, a man answered, and Robert told him, "Sir, I just spoke to your wife and told her that your son has been in a car accident." The man interrupted him with rage, yelling, "Who is this? Why are you calling me!" Robert responded by firmly stating, "Sir, calm down. Is your son Rene, does he drive a red Mustang?" He calmed down a little and said, "Yes, who is this? Why are you calling?" Robert replied, "Your son has been in a horrible accident. I don't even know if he is going to make it; you need to get to the Brownsville Hospital." The details Robert gave the man—name and vehicle, description of Rene—was enough for him to realize he was telling him the truth. Once the father believed and understood, they hung up. Robert then told Rene, "I spoke to your dad. He is going to meet you at the hospital." Rene looked relieved and told Robert, "You were calling the wrong number, right?" and then he passed out again.

12

ON THE TUGBOAT

At the time of the accident, Captain Steve Ellis resided in a condo on the main north waterway channel in Port Isabel. The night of the accident, he awoke due to a strong urge to urinate, and the timing of this urge had him awake just moments before the accidental collision of the tugboat and the causeway occurred. On his way to the bathroom, he happened to glance outside into the darkness, and he heard a long, sustained grinding and crashing sound. It was such a striking sound that it really got his attention, and he decided to see what was going on and walked down to Highway 100. As he came to the highway, he saw all manner of emergency vehicles racing toward the bridge. He went back into his condo and woke up his girlfriend, telling her what he had seen and heard and that he wanted to check it out and see if he could do anything to help. They both made their way to his truck, got inside and went to the pier to get to his boat.

Upon getting to the pier and Ellis's boat, they dropped it down into the water and made their way to Purdy's Pier. (Purdy's Pier is now the location of Pirates Landing Fishing Pier.) On the way over to Purdy's Pier, he had to deal with strong wind and a powerful current, all the while navigating in the dark. Nevertheless, he made it safely to his destination. Once he got to the pier, he encountered Dale Stockton, who had a large charter boat docked at Purdy's Pier, and it was loaded with lots of people. Ellis pulled up to the boat, which was facing toward the causeway and away from him and said, "Hey what's up?" He was met with the barrels of numerous guns and flashlights pointing toward him. The men had automatic weapons and were wearing bulletproof vests.

Everyone was yelling different orders at him, according to Captain Steve. "It was pure chaos." He had just come upon a boatload of people from just about every law enforcement agency. Steve tried to calm them down by telling them that he was there to help. Ellis said, "Not one of them knew anything about being on the water nor what to do." They were explaining to the captain that there had been a terrorist attack and that the causeway had been taken out. Some of them who really wanted to get out there and assess the situation jumped onto his boat and almost capsized it. Their sudden occupation of his boat was made even more dangerous by the fact that they had not given him a line to hold it in place, which meant the boat was not going to stay in one spot but would in fact drift away with the current. He used his experience and skill to somehow manage to keep it in its place. However, two of them just jumped right on at the same time and almost capsized the boat. They were followed by three or four more. Ellis's comment about them not knowing anything about how to act on the water was demonstrated by the haphazard method they randomly jumped onto the boat, almost sending the boat over.

Once they were settled into the boat, they asked him to take them over to the tugboat that had caused the accident. All along the way, they urged him to hurry up and go faster. Their desperation to do something immediately was driven by the belief that our country was under attack and they needed to do something to defend it. Captain Steve tried to explain to them that the waters were rough and they needed to take things easy if they and the boat were going to make it to their destination. As he approached the causeway, the first thing that drew his attention was the car that was stuck on the pylon. He could also see the taillights of the vehicles that had plunged into the water. Finally, he could see the broken causeway and the tug that had caused the accident. Some of the barges looked overloaded and he thought to himself that could have been part of what could have sent the boat onto the bridge.

As he approached the tug, he could feel the strength of the current growing stronger as they got deeper into the bay. The men began to yell at Steve, "Get me on that tugboat!" For in their minds, there were probably terrorists on board, and they needed to get to them immediately. As he approached the tugboat, he noticed that there was no line or place to tie to, so he had to maneuver his boat to bring the craft alongside the tug. An amazing feat with the strong current, but he was able to affect the maneuver and come alongside the tug. Once he came alongside, the men on board almost capsized his boat because they all tried to get on one side of the boat to get onto the tugboat. Ellis yelled, "Hold on, not all at once!" The current under the tugboat was immense. He assessed the situation, and because the tug was deeper in the water than above it, he thought maybe it had run aground (hit the bottom of the ocean).

He finally got them alongside what was the ship's galley. When they got up to the tug, they observed a long-haired individual who was making a pot of coffee. Once law enforcement got on the boat, they forced that individual to the ground, after which those who made their way onto the boat arrested everyone on board. This left no one steering the ship, causing the vessel to drift with the current. Captain Steve was thinking, "What were they doing? They need someone to be in command of their vessel." Captain Steve, seeing what was going on, told one of the officers, "OK, I am going to leave now." They responded, "No, you are going to stay here and take us back." He ignored the command because with no one at the helm of the tug, the boat could have gone with the current, hit Steve's boat and perhaps smashed into another part of the causeway. He made his way away from the tug and the accident site.[28]

Two other ship captains who assisted in the rescue effort, Todd Laurey and Daryl Steers, also made their way from Jim's Pier, which Daryl owned and where he docked a vessel. Todd had been awakened by a friend who told him about the accident and the bridge being out. Todd went to Daryl to let him know about the situation, and they decided to take the boat out to help. On the way over, they also experienced the strong current and the darkness of a lightless bridge. When they got to the barge, there were already law enforcement on board. They explained to them that they were there to help. They were tasked with taking people back and forth to the Dolphin Watch Pier, and then they were on standby.

When they arrived at the barge, they could see the captain of the ship chain-smoking and drinking lots of water, "by the gallons." They surmised that he was doing that in anticipation of having to take a drug test, which was eventually conducted. After running people back and forth, Todd was the last person tied to the barge. As he waited for the last Coast Guardsmen, whom he thought was still on board, the long-haired captain told him from the bridge that he did not have to remain there any longer. Todd responded by letting him know that he was waiting for the last Coast Guardsman. The captain's response was that he had already taken off on another boat, but if he wanted, he could come upstairs and have some coffee.

Although Todd did not drink coffee, he was curious to get on board and check out what was going on in the tug. On the bridge, he saw that in the middle of the ship's console was a television that was showing live footage from a helicopter flying above. Todd stuck his hand outside to see if it showed up and he was able to see himself. Shortly afterward, one of the deckhands ran in and said, "Did you see that? We are on TV. I'm going to get laid off this for years!" They watched the helicopter fly around and then over to the old causeway. The captain said, "Aw, those people will be fine, they have another causeway." Todd went off: "Fuck this and fuck that, that is only half a bridge! You took out the other one, how are they going to get fuel, and supplies, to the island?!" He got cut off by the captain, who said, "I believe my insurance company wouldn't want you on here, and you need to leave." He was shocked and surprised that the captain showed absolutely no remorse. When Todd got back to the pier, he was bombarded with people saying he could make fifty dollars per person to take them back and forth from the island to the mainland. Todd recalled, "No remorse on the barge, no remorse on the pier, it was unbelievable."[29]

13

BACK ON ROBERT'S BOAT

As Robert's boat approached the Port Isabel side of the bay, where the causeway connects to the city, they were met by a radiant glow of red and blue flashing lights from all the emergency vehicles that had set up camp by the Dolphin Watch Pier. It was a glow that at first was this eerie cloud of color from afar and as they approached came more into focus as the light bars on top of myriad different vehicles. When they made their way onto the dock on the mainland, they were bombarded by a large group of emergency medical technicians who immediately recognized that Rene was the most injured of the victims. They quickly worked to get him onto a backboard to properly immobilize him and prevent further injury. Once they secured him onto the stretcher, they carried him onto the pier and then on into one of their stretchers. Within minutes, a Coast Guard helicopter landed nearby, and the men disembarked and made their way over to the survivors. They took Rene and Gustavo to the helicopter, first securing Rene inside, and then tried to get Gustavo in, but the pilot was worried about the weight and sent Gustavo back to the pier with the others. Brigette was placed in a wheelchair and was rolled toward an ambulance followed by Gustavo. They were all placed in different ambulances and rushed off the scene to receive medical care and evaluation at a hospital. Chris followed each victim to their respective ambulance so that he could give a proper assessment and explanation of the nature of their injuries and what they had been through so the medics knew what to expect as they took them to the hospital.

Robert, Roland, Leroy and Tony all stood in the boat in a state of bewilderment, watching as the people they had plucked from the water and had been desperate to save were now in the hands of professionals and safe now. After a few minutes, someone walked over to them and told them to go ahead and tie the boat off to the pier, make their way over to where the causeway meets the road and wait. Someone would tend to them soon. They huddled up on a concrete slab and just stood there. The events they had just witnessed were barely beginning to settle into their minds, and they just stood there in silence as they took it all in. The silence was broken only by their heavy breathing as the adrenaline that had been pouring through their veins the entire time was finally subsiding and their breaths and heartbeats were slowing down to normal levels. However, their minds were still filled with the sights and sound of all that had transpired. Each of them replayed the images and sounds of the previous two hours. The sound of the impact, the crash of parts of the causeway slamming into the water, the hiss of the waterfall from the broken water main, the flashes of light from the snapped electrical line sweeping back and forth, the smell of gas in the water, the rocking of the boat as they tried to make their way to save the victims, the limited light of the spotlight as they made their way toward victim after victim, the screams of Gaspar and the image of the woman in the water whom they were not able to save—the trauma they would carry to this day.

14

THE PASTOR

Pastor Steven D. Hyde, of Lighthouse Assembly of God, was fast asleep in his bed when he was awoken by a call at about 2:45 a.m. One of the members of the church was Bob Harris, the fire chief, and his wife, Anita, called the pastor with great concern that Bob had not returned home from his security job at Louie's Backyard and that she had heard that the bridge had collapsed. She was worried that something had happened to him. She was hoping that maybe Pastor Hyde could find something out or just investigate what was happening. The fact that Anita Harris reached out to her pastor for assistance reveals just how close-knit the parish was and how respected Pastor Hyde was within the community. He turned over and woke up his wife. She said they better all go down there and see what they can do, so they got in their minivan and drove down to Port Isabel. They arrived, pulled over and parked in what is now the Causeway Cafe. Pastor Hyde then walked over to the staging point, which was located at the Dolphin Watch area. He arrived to find the Harris family was already there; he spoke briefly with them and led them in prayer. At the time, there were a lot of unknowns, but people were starting to think that Bob was not coming home.

He looked over and saw what appeared to be four young boys—Robert, Tony, Roland and Leroy—and thought that they had been in the accident because they looked traumatized and in shock just standing there staring off into themselves. He went over to check on them. He asked, "Did you all fall off the bridge? Were you in the accident?" Robert turned to him and asked, "I'm sorry who are you?" Hyde responded that he was "Pastor Hyde." This put Robert and the group a little at ease, and Robert replied, "No" and slowly began to tell their story, about how they had saved lives. To the pastor, their mannerisms as they told their story demonstrated the extreme state of shock that they were in, almost like they were still in the water in the thick of it. He had a word of prayer with them, asking God to come into the situation.

> Robert: Out of nowhere a man in black makes his way into our little huddle and began to talk to us. As he started talking to us and praying with us, I started to feel warm and safe for the first time since the whole event started. It also made me feel and look at what had just happened through another lens. Pastor Hyde's presence allowed us to see the hand of God in everything. The bait shop opened for us and told us where to fish. Leroy said what would happen if a car fell off the bridge. This was all God readying us for what was to come. God used the situation to touch lives. We will never know everything, but God's presence was there, and it was felt.

Pastor Hyde would later comment that "God used them that night to be fishers of men."

Hyde noticed that they were all burned in some places really bad, from the flares that they had been using, and he said, "I'll be right back; let me get you some help." Pastor Hyde called some medics to go over to check on them because he could see that Robert had been burned by the flares, to the point that his shorts had melted to his skin. EMTs attended to Robert and Roland because they were the most banged up. As Hyde and the medics talked to them, they were emotionless, with just short yes or no responses; they were severely fatigued. The pastor went on to go on and talk to authorities, thinking that these boys deserved some praise for their heroic actions.

Pastor Hyde returned, walking briskly back with some other men in tow. These men turned out to be the Texas Rangers, who abruptly took the young men into custody and removed them from the scene to the Port Isabel Police Department for questioning. Pastor Hyde was in shock as he saw them being taken away. He followed them and asked where the boys were being led to. He was just told to stay back. This was hard for the group because the pastor had become like their security blanket.

Robert: He was our father out there, and we looked back at him as they were taking us away because at that moment, he was the only one that we trusted.

Even after they were gone, Pastor Hyde kept asking where they were, and no one would tell him. Finally, he was told they were at the Port Isabel Police Department. He had formed a bond with the boys and knew they had no one else on the scene looking out for them, so he got into his van with his family and drove to the station. He tried to go in and be with them but was told that they could not have anyone in there with them. He ended up waiting outside for several hours. During this time, he ended up ministering to the people who were gathered outside the station in search of their loved ones. They really needed someone to counsel them, and he provided that for them. From his actions at the scene and his compassion, Pastor Hyde could minister to many different people, including who would never have come to the door of his church.[30]

15

THE INTERROGATION

As Robert, Leroy, Tony and Roland were escorted to the Port Isabel Police Department, they were met by a group made up of family members and friends who surmised that a loved one was in the accident. They had gathered in front of the station hoping to get some information from somebody. As Robert and company were being taken past the gathered people, some of them began yelling at them, asking them if they had seen their family members, from behind some yellow caution tape. One lady was holding up a picture of a red Mustang, which they had seen go over into the water. In fact, every car that someone asked about was one that they had seen go into the water.

> Roland: One thing that burned in my mind was the grandmother of a little blond kid "Welch" asking about a car that they did see go in, the grief on her face still hurts me. That boy lost both his parents that night. The attorneys referred to the boy as the "Golden Child"[31]

Due to the fact that he lost both his parents in the accidents, the attorneys for his family saw him as a large payout for the family and even more for themselves. Due to their involvement in the accident and the scars both inside and outside they bore, Robert and his companions would experience the legal system in all its callousness and greed. It was another added weight that these young men would have to carry with them as they made their way through life.

The first thing that drew major suspicion down on the boys was the fact that there had been a small craft advisory issued and no boats were supposed to be out on the water. In fact, the piers were all supposed to be closed. The question that the authorities had was, "What were they doing out on the water?" For there was heightened suspicion of everything because of the recent events of 9/11, which at that point was still being pieced together with no real culprit to blame and no way of knowing if there was more to come. As a result, a boat colliding with a bridge, taking the bridge out, and a group of young men in the water when no one was supposed to be in the water brought a cloud of suspicion to the youths. As soon as they got into the police station, they were all whisked away from one another and placed in different rooms for questioning.

> Robert: We weren't interrogated viciously or treated as if we were criminals. They just did their job thoroughly. They separated the four of us, and my spot was what appeared to be a little broom closet or small pantry. I waited outside as they took everything out of it as quickly as they could, just scattered everything on the floor outside, then rolled a chair into the room for me to sit on. When they put me in, they didn't close the door. I remember they didn't because I said, "Whoa, don't close the door on me I'm super claustrophobic." The male officer who was escorting me in said, "No we're going to leave it open." As soon as he said that, a lady, probably a stenographer, came in with a recording device pulled up and sat down right in front of me. The officer tells me he was with the Texas Rangers and says, "I need you to recite to her everything you did and remember from the morning of 9/11 till right now. Everything from what you ate for breakfast, lunch and dinner every day to who you visited with and where you were." I did, and it took every bit of forty-five minutes to an hour because with every statement he would ask, "Can I have that individual's full name and number?" It wasn't just a matter of, "Yeah well, I know I had oatmeal and then I went to work." It was like, "All right well when you get to work, who is the first person that you saw?" It's, pause, think okay, oh wait, no because by that point I had been up a full day before this, and this goes on for about twelve hours after we get into the Port Isabel Police Department. I was sitting there for

twelve hours reciting everything and then jotting everything down handwritten. Then another law enforcement entity came in and put a tape recorder and said, "All right go ahead and tell us everything from 9/11 till today." Eventually, I ended up giving the same statement, and answered the same questions to three different government entities, in three different fashions.

After hours of questioning, which lasted from approximately three or four o'clock in the morning until noon, the fatigue, hunger and shock had become overwhelming for Robert. By this point, all the adrenaline had worn off, which usually leads to extreme exhaustion.

Robert: I said no I'm not going to answer any more questions, man. I need to eat, and if this is the way things are going to go, I need an attorney.

Roland's wife worked for a local attorney, Frank Enriquez; after he was eventually able to call her, she, in turn, informed her boss about the fact that they were being detained and the situation with the bridge collapse. In short, the boys needed someone to look out for them legally; they were all very young and had no idea about how to purport themselves around law enforcement or how to protect themselves from any accusations.

Enriquez recognized the enormity of the situation and promptly got into his vehicle and took the one-plus-hour trip from his office in McAllen to Port Isabel. For the boys, he emerged as the hero of the day because he swooped in and rescued them from the police station and the endless questioning. At the time, he drove a big black Suburban, which had enough room for the four young men. They all climbed in, barefoot, with torn shirts, stained with blood, and burns. They were not the same boys who had piled into Robert's large red truck on their way to a night of bonding through night fishing; unfortunately, they were now bonded by a shared traumatic experience. It was only after Robert looked back from the passenger seat, the highway racing by, to see Roland asleep with his head pressed against the door, Leroy asleep leaning on Roland and Tony asleep with his head on the other door, that he knew everything was over. He could finally relax and shut his eyes. They drifted off, their mental and physical exhaustion oozing out of them, the movement and rocking of the car easing them off into slumber. For Robert, it seemed like just minutes later that they were back in McAllen. They arrived in the parking lot of the lawyer's office and found their wives waiting outside to greet them and hear their travails—finally, something familiar, a throwback to life before the tragedy.

It was three weeks later that the final and most mysterious event of that night would come into focus, answering some questions and leading to even more. They were called back to Frank Enriquez's office because they were going to be taken to be reunited with the three survivors whom they had rescued. It would be the first time that they had seen them since the night of the accident. Rene, who was the most injured from that night, was still in the hospital recovering, so the reunion would take place in his hospital room.

They arrived at Brownsville Medical Center and waited in the hallway outside of Rene's room as Rene was being attended to when his father came out of the room. He met them in the hallway. He asked, "Which one of you called me to tell me that Rene was in the accident?" Everyone turned to look at Robert, and he stepped forward, reached out his hand and said, "Hello, my name is Robert Espericueta." Rene's father grabbed his hand and pulled him in for a hug. The older man said, "You said that you spoke to my wife." Robert replied, "Yes sir, I called two times and spoke to your wife." At that moment, Robert looked toward the room for the man's wife to come out. Rene's father's eyes seemed to swell with tears, and he pointed back at the room. He struggled to get some words out and eventually said, "You see this room? My wife died in this exact room two weeks before the accident occurred." Robert could not believe the words that were coming out of his mouth; they were hitting him like a sledgehammer. He finally said, "I spoke to a lady twice when I called you." Rene's father just pulled him in and hugged him tight before releasing him. He went on to explain that he was a high school principal in Brownsville, and his initial thought when he got the call that night was that it was one of his students calling as a prank. He then turned and opened the door to Rene's room to let everyone in. Next to Rene on a small dresser adjacent to his bed was a picture of Rene's mom in a white dress. As they all walked in, they all slowly came to the realization that they recognized the woman in the picture. She was the woman whom they had all seen that night out in the water—the one they desperately tried to rescue and who brought them to where Rene was floating face down in the water. Robert's first thought as this revelation came into his head was, "A mother's love is unconditional and transcends life and death."

All those on Robert's boat, including the victims he rescued, saw the woman in the water, and when they provided testimony about that night, they all reported her presence to authorities. It is for this reason that the recovery efforts went on for three days after they had recovered all those from their vehicles. They were searching for her, but eventually, law enforcement concluded that they had indeed found everyone, and no other people were reported missing from that night. This would only reinforce the idea that it was Rene's mom who appeared that night, out of desperation to save her son. Whether it was or was not, the facts remain that they each saw a woman in the water, there were no other people missing from that night and they were shocked when they came across Rene's mom's photo there in the hospital room.

PART III

16

AFTERMATH

THE COURTS

By 3:45 p.m. the day of the accident, lawyers from Brown Water Towing had flown in on a private jet and filed a legal brief that stated that the company was valued at only $250,000. This was an effort to preempt any civil lawsuit against the company and limit its financial liability. However, as far as dealing with lawyers and the legal system, Robert, Leroy, Tony, and Roland would feel exploited by both sides, including their own attorney. It is important to understand that these were young men in their early twenties who had found themselves totally out of their element both at the accident site and in the courtroom. Their emerging post-traumatic stress disorder (PTSD) was at the time manifesting itself in anger toward the uncontrollable situation they found themselves in. They were the "other" in all the stories and in the actions of the attorneys. The means to other people's ends and their welfare were placed on the back burner to all that was going on around them. Initially, as they first entered the proceedings, they thought they were there as witnesses to the events but quickly came to the realization that they were part of a lawsuit.

> Robert: Frank Enriquez was our attorney by default. None of us really knew him; our only connection was that he was Roland's wife Hope's boss. In that sense, he lucked out

because I know he made a lot of money off this, as all the attorneys did. From day one it was a nickel-and-dime pony show on the way to each meeting or mediation that would take place at the Brownsville Federal Courthouse building. We'd be coached the whole way over there by Frank and his assistant. Both would tell us how to act, like when to be sad and to try to cry. It was all crass and ugly; they had zero consideration for the emotions that we were living, the regret, the fear, the nightmares, the night terrors. The associations we had with different things like the smell of gasoline and seeing taillights on a car lighting up as somebody pushes the brakes on a dark night. You see that, and it brings you back to that moment. They didn't seem to care at all. Every time their car hit a bump on an overpass, and we could vaguely hear an insinuation of that bump being a noise the tires make on a bridge, that the thump that you know would kind of jar us a little bit. Everybody was dealing with these things, but they seemed to think that we weren't. It was so annoying that they felt the need to coach us on how we needed to act and pretend to be distraught—we were distraught from day one. The Brownsville courthouse felt majestic. it was this creamy white building that reeked of like history.

The young men felt a certain reverence for the building and the position they found themselves in, from the security guards who checked them in to them stripping you of your phones, it gave a real sense of the formality and seriousness of it all. They walked down the corridors with the sounds of echoing shoes in the hallways and made their way to where the meetings would take place between the lawyers.

Robert: We would pass and encounter the opposing attorneys. The attorneys for the insurance company and the attorneys for Brown Water Towing. They looked like a football team of men, and each of them had an assistant, and they would wheel around these like little wire buggies with like briefcases and boxes with stacks of papers. They were intimidating, to say the least, and they all exuded wealth with everything they wore, like these top-of-the-line suits. Every crease was sewn and pressed, looking just perfect on them. While our attorneys you know were dressed in suits from Sears, trying their hardest to compete with these high-rollers. However, they couldn't, which was evident from their vocabulary and their mannerisms. We were outgunned, to say the least. I remember having this animosity toward the opposing attorneys, but I also had my own animosity with my representation. They were being driven by this money-over-people nonsense. Their sole thought was, we had to do our best to get as much money in our pocket today and that would help tomorrow. When in fact we should have been fighting for our tomorrow, not the cash today, but they didn't advise us of that. They wanted the quick buck and then moved on to the next client.

It seemed like my animosity toward my own representation would merge and be muddled along with the same animosity that I had against those that would deny us or fight to deny us what we should have gotten, which was the opposing attorneys. It became clear to me that whether you are a poor attorney or rich attorney or whether you're defending, or you know prosecuting, an attorney is a living breathing organism, and they all thrive on the potential of financial gain. "There's no justice"—they made it abundantly clear to me that justice isn't something that lives and breathes in an attorney's mind, it's the dollar signs. During our mediation sessions, we never went to an actual trial, but we would have these sessions in a courtroom with no judge because they were mediations; they acted the part of opposing teams in front of the people who lost loved ones and us. They acted like they hated each other and like one was better than the other but, in the hallways, they were all slapping each other on their shoulders, comparing shoes, advising the foreign attorneys that are here from New York, Louisiana or wherever the big company flew them in from, where they could find a good meal. All the while we had to sit there and watch all this going on in the hallway. They were all just waiting there to get to the point where checks were signed and issued. It was only about the result, financially for them. I don't remember ever feeling competently represented.

When it came to Robert, Tony, Roland and Leroy's suit filed by Enriquez, Brown Water Towing's lawyers countered with an argument based on the actual legality of their claims. Parts 8 and 9 of their briefs point out the following:

> 8. In Claimants' action, they are seeking to recover damages for emotional injuries allegedly sustained because of witnessing the partial collapse of the causeway, witnessing several automobiles fall into the water after the collapse, and participating in efforts to rescue survivors.

> 9. However, because they are unable to produce any evidence nor otherwise establish that they sustained any significant physical injury or impact, under general maritime law, the claims asserted by Claimants for purely emotional injuries are not cognizable against Brown Water.

Meaning that because there was no great physical injury, they could not make a claim for damages. They used previous examples that had come before the courts, such as *Plaisance v. Texaco*, in which the captain sued because he witnessed one of the barges he was towing collide with an underwater gas pipeline, which resulted in a large explosion. The captain subsequently engaged himself and his vessel in a rescue effort. His experience with this accident left him dealing with PTSD, and he sued for psychological damage. The ruling of the Fifth Circuit Court was that "he could not maintain his action against his employer for his purely emotional injuries." Similarly, in a similar case, the court specifically stated that "emotional injuries will be compensated when plaintiffs satisfy the 'physical injury or impact rule.'"[32] Consequently, if there was no significant physical injury, there could be no suit on purely emotional damages. This would be the argument that the young men's lawyer would be countering in court.

> Robert: In the courtroom, they always kind of floundered around one another and waited for one to say something and the other one to back it up. They brought out these big pictures of the bodies that were pulled out of the Laguna Madre, days after the accident, with no pigment and their skin just pale, white lips, and the eyelids were eaten away, chewed up by the fish and the crabs that were in the water.

For what? There was no need to do that, there was no need to bring that up, especially if it was just through mediation. The negotiations went on for four years, meeting almost once a month. Also, Frank Enriquez would get us all into his office and spend an hour talking to us about the last girl he was with or some other crazy thing that would happen. He'd bring out this tray of whiskey and pour us all drinks and we'd bullshit and literally not talk about anything pertaining to do with our case. It was all about women and money. "What are you going to do with your cut?" this and that, and keep us there for two hours. This happened about once a week. Then we would go home, and at the end of the day, he billed us for all that, all the visits where he was pouring us drinks, he billed us for them all.

I can't say if that was common practice with the other people he had represented, but that is what happened with us; he'd call us and act like he was our friend, and he would invite us to lunch. Then he would tell us that he was getting us interviews with people like Oprah. He would call us in so that we could have these powwows and huddles about how this was going to bring us stardom in some fashion and for sure it was going to bring us money. He never followed through on anything. Never made good on anything he promised. When everything was said and done, he called us and said, "Guys I got you all a great deal. If we sign this non-disclosure gag order, you each get to walk out of my office with $34,000 after my fees."

I rushed over there. I must have run two or three lights to get there as quickly as I could because I couldn't wait to get those $34,000—thirty-four grand at that time was and still is today a tremendous amount of money, and put it in the hands of a twenty-one-year-old and a compounded theoretically by a thousand and I thought holy shit. That money was gone in less than two weeks for me. I literally went to the bank because I didn't know better and cashed the check and left with a little frost bank envelope, those leather ones with the zipper on top with $34,700 in change to my house and thought that I had made it. Two weeks later, I called my therapist to ask him, "Hey man are we still on?" and he says, "No man all your funding has been pulled you can't come to see me now, you have to pay me $200 an hour." That was in a nutshell my experience after the four-year mediation. It was once lavish lunches and dinners in Brownsville. A quick, "Hey man let's go parade you guys around South Padre Island and get a bite to eat and dinner and see if you can get it for free because you guys are the heroes," to nothing. We were young and naïve, so we would go with him. He'd parade us around. Frank would walk us into a restaurant and be like "Oh these guys are the ones that saved the three survivors" and pat himself on his shoulder. He loved the attention. We did too when we were kids, and he had us right where he wanted us. He was the cool uncle that we wanted to be around during this time; years later we found out that it was just an act, a means to an end for him to get the money at the end of the day, a payday.

Frank Enriquez's demeanor and actions during the Queen Isabella Causeway Collapse case and around the young men were a sign of something deeper and darker going on with the lawyer. On October 30, 2019, agents from the Regional Child Exploitation Investigations Task Force arrived at Enriquez's law office in McAllen, Texas (he also maintained an office in San Antonio), with a search warrant, in search of child pornography. They discovered two different hard drives that contained hundreds of images and videos of children, and he was subsequently arrested. He was later released on a $100,000 bond on the condition that he would have no access to the internet and would not be allowed to be around minors, except for his grandchildren. The arrest dealt a blow to the attorney's reputation; he once had political aspirations and now he was exposed as a pedophile.[33] Likely as a result of the arrest and the exposure of his predilections, on November 11, 2019, Frank Enriquez leaped to his death off the balcony of his high-rise condo.[34]

Enriquez was not the only suicide connected to the bridge collapse. Ray Roman Marchan was one of the lead attorneys in the suits against Brown Water Towing. In 2012, he pleaded guilty to a bribery scheme in connection with a case against State Judge Able Limas. He had apparently paid over $11,000 to the judge in exchange for favorable rulings for his clients. He received a sentence of forty-two months in prison, but before he was supposed to report to federal prison, on February 28, 2013, he called a taxi to come to his house. According to testimony given to Cameron County chief deputy sheriff Gus Reyna by the taxi driver, "The passenger asked the taxi driver if he could please pull over because he was feeling nauseous and thought he was going to throw up. At that point, he exited the vehicle, climbed the rails, of the causeway, and jumped over."[35] The point from which he jumped was near where the bridge collapsed had occurred, and his body was later recovered when it washed ashore. Tragically, Marchan's daughter also took her own life by hanging herself in her home on October 17, 2013.[36] Finally, the young child who was referred to by the lawyers as the "Golden Child," Mr. Welch, passed away from an overdose of heroin on Christmas Day 2021, sparking rumors of money issues and animosity between him and his grandmother.

17

THE CITY AND RECOGNITIONS

Later that morning, residents on both sides of the bridge awoke in shock to the news of all that had transpired in the early morning hours. The sounds of the sirens from the emergency vehicles that may have stirred them in their sleep now became very real; something truly horrible had happened. The reverberations of the accident were working their way to the residents and tourists on South Padre Island. For the essential functions of the bridge were not just taking people to and from the island but also bringing goods and services to the island—not to mention the fact that the accident had taken out the water main, the power and Southwestern Bell's fiber-optic cable into the city. On top of that, there would be no garbage pick-up for over a week. These were all stressors placed on those who were stuck on the island.

That morning, many island residents assessed the situation, understood that goods would quickly become scarce on the island and formed a long line outside of the only grocery store on the island, the Blue Marlin. The store manager arrived to find the crowd waiting outside for the store to open. Within minutes of the doors opening, residents swarmed in and began to clean out the store shelves. People were grabbing large amounts of essentials, from bottled water to bread, and within minutes, the shelves of the store were laid bare. This left the manager bewildered and concerned about how he was going to be able to restock his store and keep the island fed.[37]

The only way for anyone to get on and off the next day was ship captains who turned their boats into temporary ferries and shuffled people back and forth for a fee. This proved problematic for business owners on the island. Most of the employees of the various restaurants and shops on the island did not live on the island; they came in from the mainland. This was in part because they were low-wage employees who could not afford island rents and, in turn, could not afford to pay a ship captain every day to come to work. As a result, resupply was not the only issue that business owners were facing as the city dealt with both residents and tourists.[38]

For tourists on the island, the situation was especially acute, for many of them had planned on being on the island only for the weekend and were not prepared for an extended stay. They found themselves spending a lot more money than they had planned. Additionally, many had jobs and families they needed to return to; they felt that city leaders were ignoring their plight. South Padre Island city leaders held a meeting to address the concerns of the people. The meeting quickly deteriorated for Mayor Cyganiewicz and other city officials, with tourists venting their anger toward the mayor. Nonetheless, city residents did speak up in defense of their city's leadership, reminding the tourists that they were facing an unprecedented event and that everyone was doing their best to respond to this unusual situation. Those who needed to leave the island ended up having to leave their vehicles on the island because it would take time for city leaders to negotiate the use of a ferry from Galveston.[39]

City businesses struggled for the two-and-a-half-month period before the bridge was repaired and people could once again easily drive onto the island. During the interim period, island businesses saw sales fall to 34 percent of what was usual for that time. Some businesses ended up closing their doors as they struggled to make it. Some local businesses joined the lawsuits because of the loss of jobs and revenue. Valley residents and business owners from the mainland did what they could to help promote island businesses, for they all thrived off the tourist industry and needed the island as much as the island needed them.[40] Needless to say, there was much relief when the bridge reopened for traffic.

For Robert, Tony, Leroy and Roland, the time after the accident was a whirlwind of court visits, interviews and accolades. When the story began to unfold, making its rounds through various media outlets, it immediately drew national attention. In the atmosphere of 9/11, especially immediately after the accident when it was thought to have potentially been a terrorist attack, the story certainly fit into the news cycle of the moment. The boys were interviewed by national media, but as time progressed and it was concluded that it was not a terrorist attack, the story slid to the

From left to right: Robert Espericueta, Roland Moya, Leroy Moya, unidentified and Antonio Salinas Jr. *Courtesy of Robert Espericueta.*

back burner, as the nation's interest turned back to defending itself and prosecuting those responsible for 9/11. Nonetheless, officials both local and state reached out to congratulate these young men for their actions on that tragic night.

> Roland: At first the awards were cool but then they began to become too much, and it was as if people were using them for the spotlight. They would just get the awards and then be dismissed. They were at a meeting with then Governor Rick Perry, and they were asked to leave for being too loud and when they realized who they were they were called back in.

The young men found themselves invited to different functions, and they would accept an award and then move on. The hardware chain True Value stepped up to replace all the lost fishing gear that the boys had thrown overboard during their rescue efforts. South Padre Island mayor Cyganiewicz presented the young men with keys to the city. The mayor would also go on to assist Robert with another honor.

Robert, like hundreds of others, had to leave his truck and the trailer for his boat on the island and was anxious to retrieve them once a ferry that could haul vehicles across the bay arrived in the Valley.

Above: Robert's "key to the city" from the City of South Padre Island. *Courtesy of Robert Espericueta.*

Opposite: Robert Espericueta's Certificate of Recognition by the City of South Padre Island. *Courtesy of Joshua Moroles.*

Robert: When I went to go pick up my truck and trailer, I reached out to the liaison that the mayor had appointed to us, I called her up and told her I needed to get my truck off the island. I got to the island and found that there was a line of cars from where the Sea Ranch was because that's where the ferry was, clear to Beach Access 6. Tourists, residents and workers were all trying to get off the island, but there weren't nearly enough ferries to accommodate everyone. Once I was able to get my vehicle and trailer, we were sent to the back of the line. We had a liaison for the city and for the mayor because we were doing a lot of press conferences. Our attorney was informed that I was on the beach, taking a private boat over to recover my belongings and my boat. He called the liaison to the city, and the liaison called the mayor and the mayor called the South Padre Island Police. They came and drove all the way down, knocked on my window and I'm looking at these police like "Oh my god what?" and they asked, "Are

South Padre
ISLAND, TEXAS

CERTIFICATE OF RECOGNITION

A CERTIFICATE OF THE BOARD OF ALDERMEN OF THE TOWN OF SOUTH PADRE ISLAND, TEXAS, RECOGNIZING AND THANKING MR. ROBERT ESPERICUETA FOR HIS HEROISM AND BRAVERY IN RESCUING PEOPLE AFTER THE COLLAPSE OF THE QUEEN ISABELLA CAUSEWAY

WHEREAS, commendations are in order for Mr. Robert Espericueta for rescuing victims, who, on September 15, 2001 were in danger of drowning; and

WHEREAS, a catastrophe was avoided because of the bravery and quick response to danger demonstrated by Mr. Espericueta; and

WHEREAS, this courageous act of heroism deserves special recognition by the governing body of this Town.

NOW, THEREFORE, BE IT RESOLVED BY THE BOARD OF ALDERMEN OF THE TOWN OF SOUTH PADRE ISLAND, TEXAS:

That the sincere appreciation of the Board of Aldermen, the Town Administration, and all the citizens at large of this community, is hereby extended to Mr. Robert Espericueta for his heroic action.

APPROVED ON THIS THE 23rd DAY OF SEPTEMBER, 2001.

EDMUND K. CYGANIEWICZ, MAYOR

ATTEST:

JOYCE ADAMS, CITY SECRETARY

you Robert Espericueta?" and I said, "Yes sir." He replied, "First off I would like to shake your hand, thank you for what you did." He then added, "Sir could you follow us?" They pulled me out of the line and drove me all the way past it. I was the very first car on the ferry. There is a newspaper clipping, somewhere in existence, that has the pictures of the first cars coming off the ferry, and there is my shiny red truck. It's my truck. Mayor Cyganiewicz, made that happen.

Robert's truck used the night of the accident to transport his boat. *Courtesy of Robert Espericueta.*

Two and a half months after the accident, repairs to the bridge were finally completed and the island scheduled a special event to attract tourists and Valley residents back to the island. On November 28, 2001, South Padre Island hosted a free concert by country superstar Garth Brooks. The event was planned around the Garth Brooks: Coast to Coast tour, which had been organized to promote his ninth album. The tour took Brooks from Los Angeles to Norfolk, Virginia, where he played on the deck of USS *Enterprise*, to welcome troops coming back from Afghanistan. Each concert was televised via CBS, and he was looking for a middle point for a third avenue, and South Padre became this midpoint.[41] Robert was invited to the concert, and he felt honored and excited by the fact that he was able to meet Garth Brooks.

18
THE EMOTIONAL TOLL

In interviewing Robert, especially when we are discussing specifics of the accident, you can easily see the emotional impact the event continues to have upon him. He might be looking at you when you are talking with him, but you can see the distance in his eyes as he is transported back to that night. He speaks slowly and clearly (you can hear this in the podcasts), but in his words are the details of events that are seared into his memory, events that continue to affect him in ways that he is still confronting. Albeit through maturity, time and the support of his wife, he has worked toward better dealing with it and moving forward. What follows is his side of the story, starting from when he finally made his way back home to his family.

> Robert: I remember I got home, I sat on the couch, and I retold the whole story, which I had by this time repeated over and over to authorities, to my wife, and she was both shocked and relieved at the same time because nothing had happened to me. When I was done, I went straight into my room and passed out for about thirteen or fourteen hours. After that, it was just a frenzy. Frank really was just pushing the narrative to get us, for lack of a better word, to create some kind of fandom around us, because it was the fame and money that he really wanted.

He would be like, "Hey you've got a radio show at this time, this other show at another time' "He tried to turn us into celebrities, and being young men, we ate that up. He would tell us that we needed to be seen in these specific restaurants, "So guys I'm going to make a reservation here and there and you guys need to show up and dress nicely." The whole Garth Brooks thing he really liked was being in the limelight, and without us, there was none. So, we were quickly desensitized to the trauma that we witnessed because Frank was doing such a good job distracting us from reality. Creating this kind of pitch that we would eventually be going on *Oprah* and to different networks. That we were going to be the next big thing and so he kept that up until he realized that 9/11 was going to definitively overpower what had happened. Then he just gave up on it, which was at the end of the first year after everything that happened. The second and third years afterward we would only talk to him regarding the case, and we'd go with him and meet with him during all the case-related stuff.

By the time the mediation concluded, we were spending money that we were supposedly going to have; mentally I was looking forward to a half $1 billion settlement. Where I was going to get millions, so we were expecting a lot. When the mediation concluded, I only walked away with a $35,000 check. I got disillusioned completely and realized that I put my faith and financial stability, for me and my family, in the hands of my attorney and this case. I shouldn't have, so after that, I started to develop a lot of stress issues, because I had become lazy since our attorneys were telling us that we were going to be millionaires. All we had to do was wait for the check to clear so that also made me mentally lazy. In my mind, I just must survive one more day, one more month, because eventually, the money would come in. That car that I see that guy driving and that he's worked hard for, I'm going to get it because that's what our attorneys made us believe. So, when reality hit me, I started dealing with the financial stress that I put myself in.

I started waking up with nightmares about that night, and I started having emotional relapses when I would smell the

Robert Espericueta. *Courtesy of Joshua Moroles.*

gas. It would ignite stress, then I started thinking about the height that the cars fell from, realizing holy shit man that's eighty-seven feet. It's three light poles stacked up on top of each other, and there were days when I would look at a light pole and get fixated on it. I thought wow I can't believe how big this two-ton car is coming off and falling off that height. Then, the distractions that Frank was causing us with the mediation faded, and all you're left with is the reality, and my reality was that I wasted three years of my life thinking that I was going to get rich off this thing. I was so focused on all the good things that I was going to do for myself, for my family and for my community with the money that it kept me in a positive place. But once I received the settlement, I didn't have anything positive to look forward to. All I was left with was what I experienced that night, and that's how PTSD develops. It doesn't hit you the day after it happens. It doesn't hit you even a year after it happens. Because you're distracted, and once the distractions go away and you're left with nothing but your thoughts, your memories, it fucking hits you. I didn't have that kind of thought of, oh this did this to me, or that was traumatic, until five years after the accident. To me, it was just something that happened that I was getting a lot of attention for and praise for. Praise that we're not used to getting, and now the potential of life-changing amounts of money, those things can distract you, they distracted me for five years and took me away from my responsibilities. Now dealing with my responsibilities I am stressed and what does my stress bring up at night? Memories of that night, so yeah, I didn't start feeling that magnitude of what I experienced for years.

No support, no money and no hopes, and five years of regret and shame that you weren't doing what you were supposed to be doing. In those five years, I had put all my eggs in one basket. I had dragged ass because I thought every day that I'm going to cash a check. Those of you that are pointing your fingers at me because I'm struggling are going to watch me zip by in my new expensive car. I created this future in my mind, and it was so real that I would stay there in my mind, even though I knew I was six months behind on my house. I was about to get foreclosed on, lacking at work, but the future was so bright that I didn't want to leave the reality that I had created in my mind. Once I got back to the real world, where my feet were in the present, I realized oh my gosh I'm completely fucked. Why? Because I spent too much time in my false future.

For Robert, there were plenty of signs that something was going on at the subconscious level, but as he pointed out, he was too distracted to realize that he was affected psychologically more than he knew.

After the incident, the smell of gasoline or even the sight of taillights lighting up as people press down on their brakes, would trigger something, it would put me into a state of immediate anxiety. Not so much a panic attack to where I can't breathe and I'm kind of out of control, but in the sense that my hands would get sweaty. I'd start to get a feeling of lack of oxygen flowing through my body. It would just take me back to that moment. During the process of the court hearings, it was suggested by the court and the attorneys, for those of us who witnessed what happened that night, to begin seeing a therapist. Which I did, and his suggestion was for me to begin to write things down. To document as much as I could my memories and how they made me feel at the time. Just jot down what I can.

I'll never forget what he told me, "The mind is like a safe, Robert. If you hold things in the safe, you hold them and never open the safe. You never bring the stuff out to look at it, eventually, you're going to forget what you had in it. Then you get to the age where it's difficult to unlock that safe and open it up and reminisce or look through what you left there." He said, "So you have to give it to the universe on something tangible, then you can take that tangible item and put it into a safe. You can drill it open if you must, but if you lock it up in the safe of your mind and leave it there your mind will change it, alter it, and it won't be the same." I did exactly that. I started writing it down. I started typing things down and it became a journal, then a ledger, and eventually a short little book.

The writing took place about forty to fifty days after the incident. I was living in Mission still at the same house, and I couldn't sleep, I couldn't go to work. It's weird because we as everyday people don't realize how tormenting a question just a simple question can be, like, "Why couldn't I save more or why did that person survive, and others did not? Could I have done something different?" Questions like that can eat at your soul. This therapist would tell me my mind is a super deep dark hole. It's a cubic inch wide and it seems very small, but it's the biggest, darkest hole that you can go into. If you say something that is disturbing you mentally out loud, you give it to the universe, and your ears hear it, and you'll process it differently. He said, "So I urge you to write it down because if you don't have the heart to say your fears out loud, you will not have the knowledge that you need to deal with it. Write it down and then read it out loud it'll help you to work it out." It worked for me. I put out all of those thoughts, images and feelings, onto paper. I remember he would read them to me, then ask me how I felt about them, and before long I just thought it was just like reading a book or a story that wasn't mine. I found a way to detach myself from it by hearing somebody else tell me my story. I've associated it that way since.

I can say with certainty that my memory is still very vivid. It is as accurate as it was when I first wrote it down over twenty years ago. I have had people ask me, "Well, Robert are you sure what you said is exactly what happened? Are you sure this is the way it went down?" My answer to them is always the same: this story was meant to be told even though a gag order was placed on it. I think and I don't know how it's going to come off, but I think I'm the one who was meant to tell it. I think that is why I have gone out of my way to preserve the memory of that night and now by sharing it with my children, my wife, my family members, strangers and to you.

PART IV

AFTERWARD

I first met Robert like many did, on Joshua Moroles's podcast, The True Story of the Queen Isabella Causeway Collapse. *His booming voice and matter-of-fact storytelling placed you there along with him as this amazingly tragic story unfolded. It began with what seems like a typical story of a boys' night out fishing and ended with startled, bewildered and emotionally scarred young men. The audience comes off the ride with so many questions, some that can never truly be answered, except by your own beliefs. What follows is a brief examination of some of the most extraordinary parts of this tale, the new directions the story has taken and the emotional journey Robert has been on from the moment he set foot on his ill-fated fishing trip.*

19

FATE

This tale has many themes, such as tragedy and heroism, and one of the most prevalent themes is the role of fate. Let us begin by examining the boat Robert purchased for the fishing expedition—well, not just for that day, but in the end that's what it turned out to be, an almost one-time-use vehicle. Indeed, Robert had taken the boat out only one time shortly after its purchase to try it out on the bay. In fact, on that day, he took a photo of himself and his two-year-old son, and in the background is the causeway. If this was a work of literature, that would certainly be a prime example of foreshadowing. It was his wife, Judy, who steered Robert toward the ski boat and away from a standard fishing boat; it was this choice that would allow Robert to have the room to rescue the three victims that night. Judy later remarked to me in an interview that the boat had "served its purpose," which I feel is an apt description for the role the boat played in this extraordinary tale. For the boat was never used by Robert again. Physically, the boat was battered, scraped up and bloodstained, and there was also the horrible connection to the collision and chaos of that night. It ended up being auctioned off at a loss; however, it was not really a loss, for it was a tool that was needed that night to "save."

Moreover, Robert points out that there was absolutely no alcohol on the boat that night, a fact that he admits was rather unusual for his group, probably a product of fatigue or a rush to pack to get out on the road. Being sober allowed them to act as calmly as they did and for them to have to the forethought to quickly empty the boat of its contents so that they could have enough room to rescue as many people as possible—a small detail, but one whose importance must be recognized as playing a role in the rescue.

Next, we have the events that took place at the Quick Stop bait shop. The boys arrived just after closing, and the tired employee who did not want to open for the boys. Whether it was out of frustration, perhaps thinking that it would be quicker to give them what they need than sit there and argue with them, he did open for Robert and company. We also had Robert—who is always one to be friendly and attempt to make everyone calm and relaxed around him—decide the best way he could cool the employee down was to distract him with a conversation. He asked about the best place to do some night fishing, a question that, whether Robert was aware of it or not, was a way to also give back control of the situation to the employee. Robert now appeared to look toward the expertise of the worker, and the worker responded with what was a most fortuitous suggestion: tying themselves to one of the pillars and fishing from there. Though it served the purpose of calming down the employee, Robert dismissed the suggestion because he already had a plan for where he was going to go that night and was not tying his boat to a pier. In the end, that is exactly where he found himself that night.

Furthermore, we have the role of time in the whole situation. In studying accidents, one comes to understand that an accident is never a product of one single event or issue, mechanical or human, but a series of things that happen without which one could be subtracted and nothing would have ever happened. Time did play a role in the accident itself; however, in this examination, we will be considering the factor time played in the boys' role as rescuers that night. That night, there were several pieces of timing crucial to the eventual rescue. To begin with, there is the fact that none of the wives had time to pay attention to the news, specifically the weather, where the small craft advisory was issued. The only person who apparently had was Robert's sister, and he was not about to listen to her, especially because she called while Robert was still near the shore and was not feeling the full effects of the intense current that was flowing that night. At the same time, you have the issue with the boat and Robert and the boys' unfamiliarity, which led to them having to stop for some time to determine just why it was spurting water. This delay placed them under the bridge at a certain time and slightly away from the causeway when the collision happened. If they had not been delayed, they may have grown tired or bored and left the area altogether, but they were precisely where they were supposed to be at the time that they needed to be in that specific spot in the water.

Then, you also have the almost morbid conversation among the boys about cars falling from the bridge. What would they do? Robert's initial and honest response to the question would be to do nothing and head home, which, when the accident did happen, was indeed his initial reaction. He has pointed out that the conversation they had concerning a possible accident happening before them was a way to prepare them for all that was to transpire that night. So, one can certainly wonder whether that thought was planted in Roland's mind for that purpose or just a thought brought about by the constant thumping of the cars crossing over their heads from the causeway above. This is a case of opinion, but the fact is that the conversation did indeed take place.

Perhaps the most extraordinary part of this tale, and one that is also controversial, is the role of the woman in white in the water. There are certain facts associated with this part of the story, but beyond that, it is up to your personal beliefs as to what you surmise happened. The facts are in plain black and white: the statements provided by Robert, Tony, Roland and Leroy to the investigators. (The Texas Ranger affidavits are provided in the appendix of this work.) Her appearance in the middle of the rescue effort undeniably drew them to find Rene, who was already floating face down in the water, which meant that he needed to be brought out of the water as fast as possible before he drowned. What the young men saw that night is the subject of much speculation in all who have heard the story. For some, it is just as simple as a mother's love knowing no bounds, piercing even the veil between this world and the afterlife. Those of us who are parents know that the hopes and dreams we possess for our children do not end when our life ends but will always be there to guide them and push them to complete their life's vocation. Whether it is by our memory in their minds or a fear of disappointing us even after we are gone, or us truly watching over them, we believe we are there for them. This may be what the young men saw that night, a manifestation of a mother's desire to save her son so that he could live on and become the man she hoped he would be. But for others who do not want to lean on some sort of supernatural explanation, it remains a mystery. An enduring question, but what is a fact is that those on the boat all saw the same thing and rendered what they saw to authorities in their statements. The Coast Guard searched long and hard for the woman in the water. In the end, after verifying that no other person was reported missing, they gave up the search for the mysterious woman. The final big reveal in the hospital room and the shock of all those present who had seen her in the water provided even further proof that those on board did have a shared perhaps "spiritual" experience.

In keeping with the subject of a shared spiritual experience, there was the encounter with Pastor Hyde. He was there right when the young men needed someone to help them come down from the adrenaline-fueled past hours. When one is in the middle of something as traumatic and chaotic as the whole incident was, there is a tendency to remain sharply focused on the "now" and what you are doing right at that very moment. Even when the Coast Guardsmen, Chris, took over piloting Robert's boat, he was not free from the situation but turned to attend to the injured aboard his boat. Leroy, Roland and Tony were focused the whole time, either pulling the victims out, talking to them, reassuring them or attending what they could with the little rescue equipment and spare clothing they had. They were living in the moment. However, once they made it to the Port Isabel side of the bay and were on the mainland, their minds and hearts were now racing with all they had just witnessed and been a part of, and this was where they mentally needed someone to lean on. After all, these were just young men who had no experience in anything like this—they did not choose to be a first responders—they were just boys doing what they could to help. So it was at this time when they needed comfort and guidance that they were met by Pastor Hyde. He met with the boys and became the parent in the room that they so desperately needed. He offered them prayers and comfort and tried to impart to them the enormous amount of good they had done, explaining that they were acting as God's instruments. Hyde explained to them that although they had been out on the water fishing for fish, he had made them "fishers of men."

20

JOSH, ROBERT AND THE BRIDGE TODAY

Robert and Josh's friendship has come a long way since their fortuitous meeting at Robert's Poker House. You can see it in all their interaction with each other, whether it is on their YouTube channel, podcasting or in person. They have gone on to produce an award-winning documentary on the incident titled *The Collapse*. They shopped this documentary around the country and won recognitions in festivals, including "Best Feature Film" at the Gulf Coast Film & Video Festival, "Best Documentary" at the New Jersey Film Awards and "Best Feature Documentary" at the New York Movie Awards, just some of the accolades the film has received. The traveling to and from these festivals has really brought these two remarkable men together, and they are currently embarking on other endeavors, such as the launch of their production company Studio 4240.

Studio 4240 hosts a variety of platforms and services, most of which promote Rio Grande Valley businesses and issues of concern in the region. However, they are already embarking on their next film project, currently titled *Conquista* about the defacing of Picasso's 1932 *Woman in a Red Armchair* by Uriel Landeros in 2012. Landeros, who was twenty-two at the time, entered the Menil Museum in Houston, Texas, and managed to stencil an image of a bullfighter, a bull and the word *Conquista* over Picasso's work. The men are looking to explore his reasoning for the act and the impact it has had in the art community. These men are not just sitting on their laurels,

Above: Robert Espericueta and Joshua Moroles. *Courtesy of Joshua Moroles.*

Opposite: Robert Espericueta and Juan Carmona at the Cinesol Film Festival. *Courtesy of Juan Carmona.*

and in their telling of the story of the causeway collapse, they have found a passion for storytelling and promoting stories from the Rio Grande Valley.

As for the Queen Isabella Causeway, it is still the main method of entering South Padre Island, and the island itself is still a major tourist attraction for the public and spring breakers. The bridge itself has had some upgrades, which are a direct result of the 2001 collapse, as well as a similar collapse in 2002 at Webbers Falls, Oklahoma. The collapse and Webbers Falls were also due to a towboat pushing a barge and colliding with a bridge, collapsing a section of it. These incidents led the Texas Department of Transportation (TxDOT) to create a collapse warning system. According to the Federal

Above, top: The memorial to the accident. *Courtesy of Joshua Moroles*.

Above, bottom: The plaque on Gustavo Morales's memorial bench. *Courtesy of Joshua Moroles*.

Highway Commission, the system includes: "A continuous fiber optic cable for signal transmission. A controller to monitor the signal. Traffic gates, dynamic message signs, and warning signs. A telephone auto-dial system." This system "works by detecting the loss of a signal that is transmitted over fiber optic cable. A controller monitors the signal and activates motorist warnings if the signal is lost. A telephone auto-dial system then notifies TxDOT and emergency personnel." It also uses a system of signal lights and signage to warn motorists of the collapse so that they can recognize

Gustavo Morales sitting on his memorial bench. *Courtesy of Joshua Moroles.*

the danger and stop their vehicles before they make it to the broken section. TxDOT also conducts routine safety checks of the system to ensure that all equipment is in working order.[42] The presence of such a system will hopefully save lives, but it is also to be hoped it will never have to be used.

As we conclude this story, we must recognize those who lost their lives on that tragic September night. There is a naval tradition that has been passed on to merchants and fishermen of ringing a bell as the names of those lost at sea are read. So perhaps as you read these names you can project the sound of a bell ringing solemnly as you read each name. They are as follows:

Robert Victor Harris, age forty-six
Gaspar Saenz Hinojosa, age fifty-two
Robin Faye Leavell, age twenty-nine
Hector Martinez Jr., thirty-two
Julio Cesar Mireles, twenty-two
Stvan Francisco Rivas, age twenty-two
Barry R. Welch, age fifty-three
Chelsea Louise Welch, age twenty-three

NOTES

1. *Merriam-Webster*, "Humanity."
2. State of Texas Comptroller's Office, "South Texas Region."
3. Moroles, interview.
4. Ibid.
5. Ibid.
6. Ramirez, "New Environmental Study."
7. National Park Service, "Padre Island."
8. Lipscomb, "Karankawa Indians."
9. Hathcock, "Rio History."
10. National Transportation Safety Board, "N63166T Accident Description."
11. Ramirez, "New Environmental Study."
12. Hartig and Doherty, "Two Decades Later."
13. Mills, "Twenty Years."
14. Graff, "After 9/11."
15. United States Coast Guard, *Formal Investigation*.
16. Ibid.
17. Ibid.
18. Moroles, "Captain Steve Ellis."
19. United States Coast Guard, *Formal Investigation*.
20. Ibid.
21. Ibid.
22. Moroles, "Gustavo Morales."
23. Moroles, "Roland Moya."

24. Moroles, "Tony Salinas."

25. Ibid.

26. Moroles, "Gaspar Hinojosa II."

27. Moroles, "EMS Hero JP Montoya."

28. Moroles, "Captain Steve Ellis."

29. Moroles, "2 Boat Captains."

30. Moroles, "Queen Isabella—Pastor Hyde."

31. Moroles, "Roland Moya."

32. *Petitioners Brown Water Marine Service*, private papers of Robert Espiricueta.

33. "Prominent South Texas Attorney Arrested," *Progress Times*.

34. "Attorney Commits Suicide," *Advance News Journal*.

35. Bezosky, "Convicted Attorney's Body Washes Ashore."

36. Horta, "Daughter of Attorney."

37. CBS 4 News Rio Grande Valley, "KGBT Archives: Run On Groceries."

38. Ibid.

39. Ibid.; "KGBT Archives: Tourists Stranded by SPI Causeway Collapse."

40. CBS 4 News Rio Grande Valley, "Getting Back to Business"; Newson6, "South Padre Island Officials Hope Garth Brooks Concert will Reinvigorate Economy."

42. Department of Transportation: Federal Highway Administration "Showcasing an Advanced Motorist Warning System in Texas."

BIBLIOGRAPHY

Advance News Journal. "Attorney Commits Suicide: How the Peer-to-Peer Software Facilitates." November 26, 2019. www.anjournal.com.

Bezosky, Lynn. "Convicted Attorney's Body Washes Ashore." March 1, 2013. www.mysanantonio.com.

CBS 4 News Rio Grande Valley. "Getting Back to Business on South Padre Island." YouTube. www.youtube.com.

———. "KGBT Archives: Run On Groceries Due to Causeway Collapse." YouTube. www.youtube.com.

———. "KGBT Archives: Tourists Stranded by SPI Causeway Collapse." YouTube. www.youtube.com.

Department of Transportation: Federal Highway Administration. "Showcasing an Advanced Motorist Warning System in Texas." November 2012.

Graff, Garett M. "After 9/11, the U.S. Got Almost Everything Wrong." *The Atlantic*, September 8, 2021. www.theatlantic.com.

Hartig, Hannah, and Carroll Doherty. "Two Decades Later, the Enduring Legacy of 9/11." Pew Research Center. September 2, 2021. www.pewresearch.org.

Hathcock, Steve. "Rio History: A Brief History of the Queen." *Port Isabel Press*, July 1, 2020. www.portisabelsouthpadre.com.

Horta, Joey. "Daughter of Attorney Who Committed Suicide Takes Her Own Life." October 17, 2013. www.valleycentral.com.

Lipscomb, Carol A. "Karankawa Indians." *Handbook of Texas Online*, November 13, 2020. www.tshaonline.org.

Merriam-Webster Dictionary. "Humanity." www.merriam-webster.com.

Mills, Kim. 2021. "Twenty Years after 9/11, What Have We Learned about Collective Trauma? with Roxane Cohen Silver, PhD." *Speaking of Psychology*, episode 157. www.apa.org.

Moroles, Joshua. "Captain Steve Ellis Perspective of What Happened on the Water That Night." YouTube. www.youtube.com.

———. "EMS Hero JP Montoya Talks About His Experience Saving Gaspar Hinojosa on That Queen Isabella Pillar." YouTube. www.youtube.com.

———. "Gaspar Hinojosa II, Son of the Man Who Fell on the Pillar of the Causeway, Joins Us." Episode 4. YouTube. www.youtube.com.

———. "Gustavo Morales, 1 of 3 Survivors of the Queen Isabella Causeway Collapse." YouTube. www.youtube.com.

———. Interview by Juan Carmona. January 5, 2022.

———. "Queen Isabella—Pastor Hyde." YouTube. www.youtube.com.

———. "Roland Moya, The Other Fisherman on the Boat, Joins Us." YouTube. www.youtube.com.

———. "Tony Salinas, the Other Fisherman on the Boat, Joins Us." Episode 6. YouTube. www.youtube.com.

———. "Tony Salinas, the Other Fisherman on the Boat, Reads His Affidavit." YouTube. www.youtube.com.

———. "2 Boat Captains Talk About What They Experienced Hours After the Bridge Collapse." YouTube. www.youtube.com.

National Park Service. "Padre Island: Geologic Formations." www.nps.gov.

National Transportation Safety Board. "N631667T Accident Description." https://planecrashmap.com.

Newson6.com. "South Padre Island Officials Hope Garth Brooks Concert Will Reinigorate Economy." www.newson6.com.

Petitioners Brown Water Marine Service, INC. and Brown Water Towing, INC.'s Motion for Summary Judgement on Claims Asserted by Certain Claimants Who Sustained No Physical Injury or Impact Filed in the United States District Court for the Southern District. 2002. C.A. No. B-01-157 (United States District Court for the Southern District of Texas Brownsville Division, May 28).

Progress Times. "Prominent South Texas Attorney Arrested on Child Pornography Charge." November 12, 2019. www.progresstimes.net.

Ramirez, Marco. "New Enviromental Study for Possible Second Causeway on SPI." July 21, 2021. www.valleycentral.com.

State of Texas Comptroller's Office. "The South Texas Region: 2020 Regional Report." 2020. https://comptroller.texas.gov.

United States Coast Guard. *Formal Investigation into the Circumstances Surrounding the Allison Between the Barge Tow of the M/V* Brown Water V *and the Queen Isabella Causeway Bridge on September 5, 2001. In Port Isabel, Texas, Resulting in Multiple Loss of Life.* 2005.

ABOUT THE AUTHORS

Juan P. Carmona is a social studies teacher at Donna High School and a dual enrollment history instructor through South Texas College. A member of the award-winning Refusing to Forget Project and the Hidalgo County Historical Commission, he is the author of *The Alton Bus Crash* and *The Deadly 1940 Alamo Train Crash*, co-host of *Mi Valle Mi Vida* and producer (with his Mexican American history students) of *The Alamo Train Crash of 1940* podcast.

Robert Espericueta stands as a testament to the power of storytelling, seamlessly blending his roles as an entrepreneur, speaker and scriptwriter. With a career crowned by numerous accolades, Robert has carved a unique niche in the world of documentary filmmaking and scriptwriting. His directorial debut, *The Collapse*, along with his second critically acclaimed film, *Conquista*, marked twenty years of unwavering dedication, patience and artistic vision finally brought to life.

An award-winning scriptwriter, Robert's talent for crafting engaging and thought-provoking stories is renowned. His work is characterized by a deep understanding of the human experience, which he translates into scripts that resonate with and move his audience. Beyond his achievements in film and writing, Robert is known for his skills as a prolific speaker, eloquently connecting with people and inspiring others in the art of storytelling.

Now, with two powerful documentaries under his belt and a life rich in experiences, Robert Espericueta stands at the pinnacle of his storytelling prowess. His continued work and deep appreciation for the arts inspire and influence a wide audience, proving that a well-told story can indeed change the world.

Visit us at
www.historypress.com